Tiny treasure

Adorable Crochet Keychain Patterns

Table of Content

01 Introduction — 1

02 Abbreviation — 2

03 All You Need to Know Before Crocheting — 3

04 Crochet techniques and stitches — 8
How to how a crochet — 9
Beginners Crochet Basic Stitches — 11

05 Cute Keychains patterns — 16
Basic patterns — 17

Table of Content

05 Cute Keychains patterns — 16

Basic patterns — 17
Cute Crochet Keychain Wristlet — 18
Aldi Quarter Keeper — 20
Unicorn Earbud Holder — 22
Santa lip balm holder — 29

Animal keychain patterns — 17
Cat Keychain — 36
Koala Keychain — 38
Fish keychain — 40
Rabbit Keychain — 43

Fruits and food keychain patterns — 47
Mandarin Keychain — 48
Avocado Keychain — 50
Lemon Keychain — 53
Apple Keychain — 58

Table of Content

05 **Cute Keychains patterns**   16
Fruits and food keychain patterns   47
Strawberry keychain   62
Mini pumpkin keychain   66
Pizza Keychain   68
Taco Keychain   72
Other keychain patterns ideas   78
Camera keychain   79
Sun Keychain   81
Toadstool Sweater Keychain   84
School bus keychain   87
Roller Skate Keychain   92

Introduction

Introducing 'Tiny Treasures: A Crochet Guide to Adorable Keychains'! If you've ever wanted to add a touch of handmade charm to your daily routine or create delightful gifts for friends and family, this is the perfect guide for you. This book is designed to help you craft adorable keychains that are both fun to make and lovely to use.

Whether you're new to crochet or have been stitching for years, these projects are perfect for you. We've included a wide range of patterns, from cute animals and whimsical characters to elegant motifs and playful designs. Each project comes with detailed, easy-to-follow instructions and clear illustrations to guide you every step of the way.

Crocheting these tiny treasures is a wonderful way to relax, unleash your creativity, and produce something truly special. Imagine the joy of attaching a cute little crochet creation to your keys, bag, or gifting it to someone special. These keychains aren't just accessories; they're expressions of your love for crafting and the unique touches that make life a little brighter.
So grab your yarn and hook, and let's dive into the world of "Tiny Treasures." Happy crocheting!

Abbreviation

Abbreviation	Crochet Action
alt	alternate
beg	begin(ning)
bet	between
con or cont	continue
dec	decrease
foll	follow(s)(ing)
inc	increase
lp	loop
patt	pattern(s)
rem	remain(s)(ing)
rep	repeat(s)(ing)
RS	right side
sc	simple crochet

Abbreviation	Crochet Action
*x	repeat x times
slst	slipstitch
sk	skip
sp	space(s)
TBL	through back loop, or turning back loop
TFL	through front loop, or turning front loop
tog	together
WS	wrong side
yo	yarn over
hdc	half double crochet
ch	chain

Decrease (sc2tog): Insert hook into a stitch, draw up a loop. Insert hook into next stitch, draw up a loop. Yarn over, and draw through all 3 loops on the hook.
Decrease (sc3tog): Insert hook into a stitch, draw up a loop. Insert hook into the next stitch, draw up a loop, repeat once more. Yarn over, draw through all 4 loops on the hook.

ALL YOU NEED TO KNOW BEFORE CROCHETING

01 WHAT IS CROCHET?

Crochet is the art of creating fabric by looping yarn with a crochet hook. It might sound simple, and it actually is! However, learning to crochet takes time and patience, so take it slow. Remember, you'll probably make mistakes along the way, but that's perfectly okay. Be sure to read through all the sections below to get started.

02 WHAT MATERIALS OR TOOLS DO I NEED TO CROCHET?

While, you'll really only need just two basic crochet supplies as a beginner to get started, we also have a full list of our recommended products like scissors, stitch markers, yarn needles and more.

- Yarn: Yarn comes in many weights (how thick it is) and yardages. Certain projects use specific weights of yarn, but others – like blankets – can use just about any weight. You can buy yarn online or in-store, but I always prefer to buy it online. Online, you have a much wider selection and can choose from just about any brand there is.
- Scissors: A great pair of stork scissors will get the job done, and these should be considered your crochet only scissors, so don't let anyone else use them for anything else.
- Stitch markers: These are great for marking your stitches in projects and keeping track of rows.
- Tapestry needle: These will help you to weave in all the loose yarn ends at the end of your project. They can be sometimes referred to as yarn needles.

02

WHAT MATERIALS OR TOOLS DO I NEED TO CROCHET?

- **Crochet Hook:** Crochet hooks come in many sizes. The most common, however, is anywhere between a 3 mm and 15 mm size. There are sizes smaller and larger than those, but are only used for very specific use cases. Crochet hooks are generally used with specific yarn weights as well. For example, medium #4 weight yarn should be used with either a 5.5 mm or 6.5 mm hook.
- With the variety of yarns and hooks available, the choices can feel overwhelming. Fortunately, nearly every crochet pattern provides the details you need.
- No need to stress... the pattern will specify the exact yarn weight, type of yarn, and recommended hook size. Armed with the right yarn and hook, you'll be ready to start making your first scarf, hat, blanket, or any other beginner-friendly project you choose.

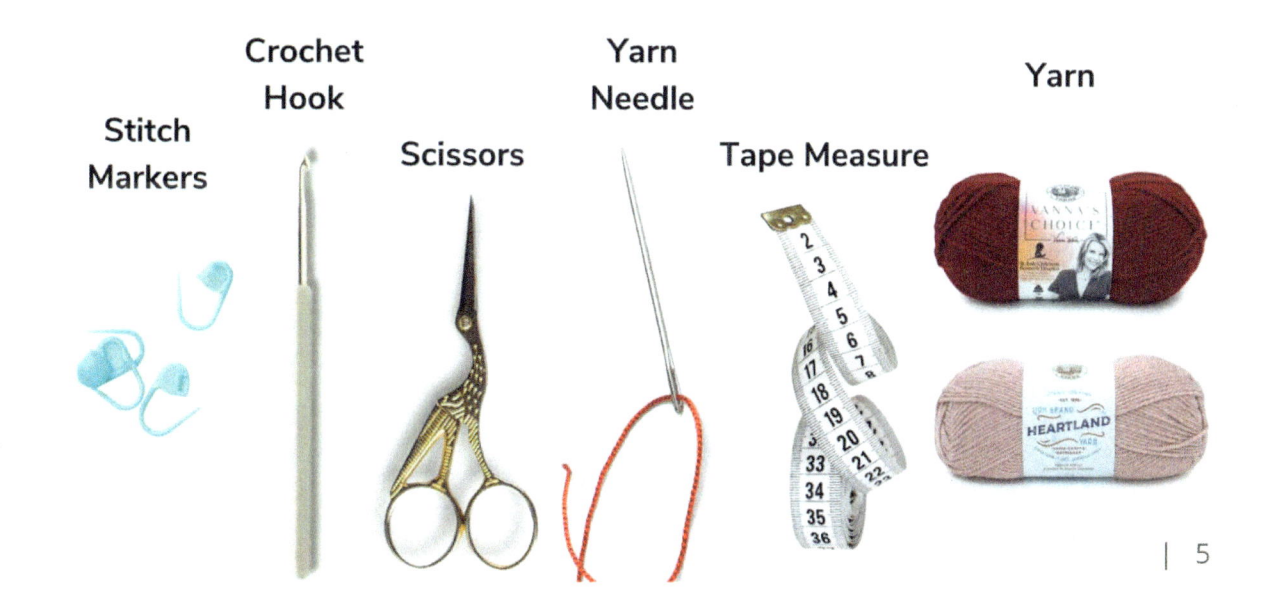

Stitch Markers

Crochet Hook

Scissors

Yarn Needle

Tape Measure

Yarn

| 5

03 WHAT IS A CROCHET HOOK?

A crochet hook is a handheld tool used to create crochet stitches. This image outlines the various parts of a crochet hook, including the point, throat, grip, shaft, and handle. It's essential to get to know your crochet hook, so when you first pick one up, you'll understand its components. This knowledge will help you as you start crocheting and begin your first pattern.

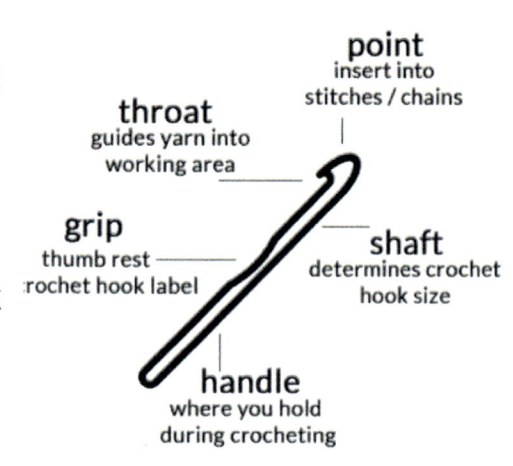

point — insert into stitches / chains
throat — guides yarn into working area
grip — thumb rest / crochet hook label
shaft — determines crochet hook size
handle — where you hold during crocheting

04 CROCHET HOOK SIZES

There are over thirty different sizes of crochet hooks, and crochet patterns will usually require a specific hook size.
Crochet hooks are identified by either their US or Metric names. For example, a 5.5 mm metric size hook is also called a I-9 size hook in the US.

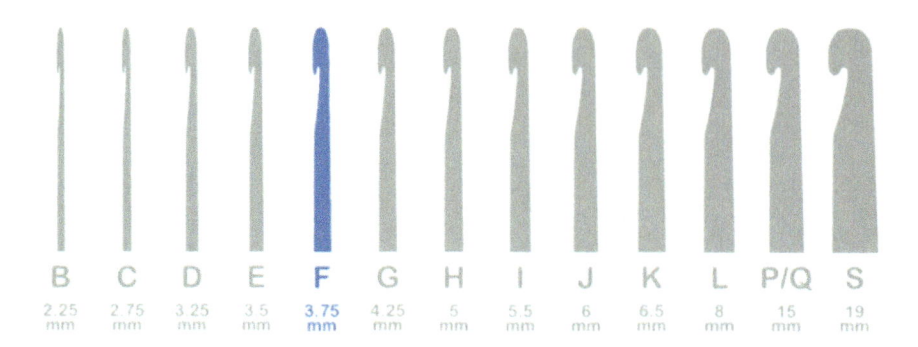

B	C	D	E	F	G	H	I	J	K	L	P/Q	S
2.25 mm	2.75 mm	3.25 mm	3.5 mm	3.75 mm	4.25 mm	5 mm	5.5 mm	6 mm	6.5 mm	8 mm	15 mm	19 mm

05 YARN IN CROCHET

Yarns come in various fibers, lengths, and weights, and you can identify a yarn's characteristics by reading its label. Yarn thickness, which determines its weight, is classified into numerical categories from 0 to 7.

The yarn's weight also dictates the size of the crochet hook you'll need. To simplify things, most yarn companies provide this information on the label of each skein. So, if you're ever unsure about the yarn's weight or the appropriate hook size, just check the label.

5 SKEIN WEIGHT — How much the yarn skein weighs in grams or ounces

6 YARN WEIGHT — A number from 1-7 indicating the thickness of the yarn

7 GAUGE — Recommended hook size to achieve preferred stitches per inch

4 SKEIN LENGTH — The total yards or meters of yarn in the skein

3 FIBER CONTENT — The material of the yarn

8 CARE DIRECTION — How to wash and dry for your finished project

| 7

CROCHET TECHNIQUES AND STITCHES

HOW TO
HOLD A CROCHET HOOK

The 5 Design Features of a Crochet Hook

It's helpful to understand each part and its purpose so you can hold your hook confidently and don't form bad habits that could stymie your enjoyment or cause you pain with repeated movement. Please refer to the illustration below as you read the following descriptions:

A] The hook: The design feature that gives this utensil its name and allows you to hook those pretty stitches.
B] The throat: a tapered feature that helps you slide your stitch up to...
C] The working area: a thicker feature and the site of all stitch creation.
D] The finger hold or thumb rest: the flattened feature that gives you a good grip on your hook.
E] The handle: the feature that provides a resting place for your fourth and fifth fingers and overall balance to your hand.

Parts of a Crochet Hook

NOTE: You know the old adage: location location location! So remember to make every stitch on the working area [C] of your hook. If you were to make a stitch on the throat [B], it would come out too tight.

If you were to make a stitch on the finger hold [D], it would stretch the stitch and make it too loose. See? Super important to understand the five design features of a crochet hook so you know where on the hook to make your stitches and why that matters!

HOW TO
HOLD A CROCHET HOOK

Knife Grip vs Pencil Grip in Crochet

If you're still a beginner, then you may want to try each way and see what feels better to you. If you've been crocheting for years and wanting to see if the other grip might work better for you, give it a try.

The Knife Grip

To achieve the knife grip, hold the thumb rest [D] with your thumb and third finger while your pointer finger stretches along the back of the working area [C].

The Pencil Grip

To achieve the pencil grip, hold the thumb rest [D] between your thumb and pointer finger and let your third finger rest along the back of the working area [C].

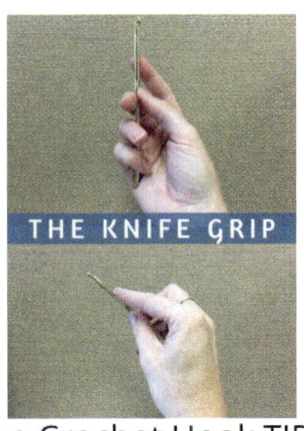

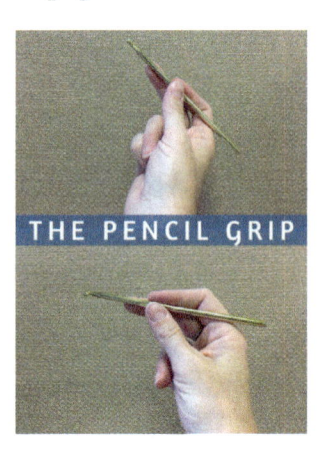

How to Hold a Crochet Hook TIPS:
1. The knife grip is often the most comfortable, but try different grips to find what feels best.
2. Always face the hook [A] towards you.
3. Hold the hook firmly but not too tightly. Your hand may be tense initially, but it will relax with practice.

BEGINNERS CROCHET BASIC STITCHES

A crochet stitch is a result of moving a crochet hook through yarn to achieve a specific shape and look in your crochet pattern. Its abbreviation is st for a single stitch and st(s) for more than one stitch. A stitch is a series of specific movements made with yarn on your crochet hook that will result in a finished stitch. It can be one movement or many movements, depending on what you are crocheting.

Crochet stitches with distinctive names tend to resemble the name. One shell stitch looks like one shell, one v stitch looks like a "v," and one popcorn stitch looks like a piece of popcorn.

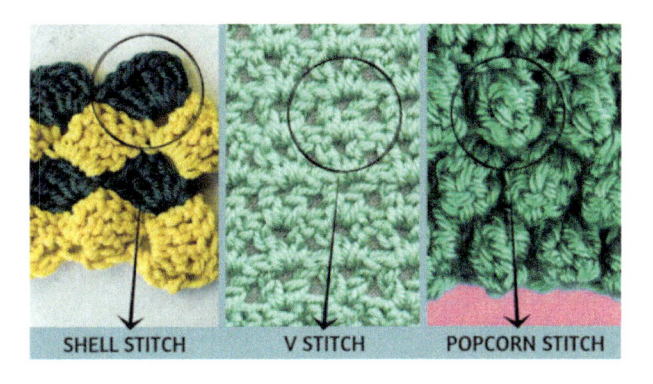

SHELL STITCH   V STITCH   POPCORN STITCH

SINGLE CROCHET   DOUBLE CROCHET   TRIPLE CROCHET

Those distinctive stitches are easier to see. The basics, like single crochet, double crochet, triple (treble) crochet, and half double crochet are not as easy to distinguish but you can easily see that they get larger in size.

SLIP STITCH

A slip stitch is more of a place holder technique used to aid other stitches in a pattern.

BEGINNERS CROCHET BASIC STITCHES

1. Chain Stitch (ch)
A chain stitch, is a simple crochet stitch that often forms the foundation of what crochet stitches are worked into during most crochet projects.

The number of chains across in a crochet pattern can determine the length or the width of a crochet project.

1. To make your first stitch, start by making a slip knot.
2. Insert hook into slip knot point first, bring yarn over the shaft of the hook from back to front and grab it with the throat of the hook.
3. Draw hooked yarn through slip knot and onto the hook. This movement will make one ch stitch.
4. Repeat steps two and three for the next stitches until you have the desired number of stitches for a pattern. One loop will remain on hook.

2. Single Crochet Stitch (sc)
One single crochet stitch after another creates a tighter crochet fabric in projects and is the perfect stitch for beginners for easy crocheting.

1. Insert the crochet hook from front to back in the center of the second chain from the hook.
2. Bring the yarn over (**yo**) the hook and pull the yarn back through the chain from back to front (2 loops on hook).
3. Yo and pull through both loops on the hook.
4. Learn more about the single crochet stitch and how to start making single crochet rows for your next project.

BEGINNERS CROCHET BASIC STITCHES

The Steps
Step 1: Chose your yarn
Step 2: Chose the hook that corresponds to the yarn (that can be found on the **yarn label**)
Step 3: Hold the hook in your dominant hand (left hand or right hand), Make a slip-knot and chain 10 (or whatever amount you'd like)

Step 4: In the second chain stitch from the hook

Step 5: Wrap the yarn over the hook, and pull it back through the chain. This will create one loop on the hook. You will now have two loops on the hook.

BEGINNERS CROCHET BASIC STITCHES

The Steps (Single Crochet Stitch (sc))
Step 6: Wrap the yarn over the hook again, and pull it through both loops on the hook. You have completed your first single crochet stitch.

Step 7: Single crochet into each chain across, At the end of the row, chain 1 and turn your work aka flip over, Chain 1 and repeat steps 6-8 to complete another row.

3. Slip Stitch (sl st)
A slip stitch is a stitch that used in surface crochet as well as in patterns to create texture and uniqueness.
1. Insert hook into the designated stitch
2. YO and pull back through the st and through the loop on the hook.

4. Half Double Crochet Stitch (hdc)
The half double crochet stitch or HDC stitches are a favorite stitch of many since it has some height but is also quick to work up.
1. Yo (yarn over) insert the hook from front to back of the designated stitch
2. Yo the hook and pick up a loop.
3. Yo the hook and pull back through all three loops on the hook.
4. You have now completed a half double crochet stitch.

Half Double Crochet

BEGINNERS CROCHET BASIC STITCHES

5. Double Crochet Stitch (dc)
Double Crochet stitches are fun to learn because it's the next step up from a half double crochet. You'll quickly realize how much quicker it is to finish crochet projects when you are using double crochet stitches over the other types of stitches.

1. Wrap the yarn over the hook, insert the hook into the specified st.
2. YO the hook again, draw the yarn through the st, so there are 3 loops on the hook
3. YO the hook again draw it through 2 loops, so there are 2 loops on the hook
4. YO the hook, draw it through the final 2 loops.

6. Triple Crochet Stitch (tr)
The Triple Crochet stitch or Treble Crochet Stitch (aka treble stitch), one of the tallest crochet stitches you can create. This is usually the next stitch you'll want to learn after the DC stitch.

1. Make a chain of a desired length of any #
2. Yarn over the hook twice, insert hook in the designated the next stitch (the fifth chain from the hook for the first TR of a project)
3. YO, draw through the stitch (four loops on the hook)
4. YO, draw yarn through two loops on the hook. (three loops on the hook)
5. YO, draw yarn through two loops on the hook (two loops on hook)
6. YO, draw yarn through two loops on the hook

CUTE KEYCHAINS PATTERNS

Practical keychain patterns

Cute Crochet Keychain Wristlet

Materials

- 13 – 15 yards of Dishie cotton yarn (held double) [I used Verdigris, Azure, and Mulberry]
- or 13 – 15 yards of a similar #4 worsted weight cotton yarn (held double)
- J 6.0 mm crochet hook
- 1.2 inch flat keyring or swivel lobster clasp with 1 inch D ring
- Tapestry needle
- Scissors

Gauge / Size

- Gauge: 4 x .75 inches = 1 row of 11 ldc
- Flat Size: 11 inches long x .75 inches wide
- Folded Size: 5.5 inches long x .75 inches wide

Pattern Notes

- ch-3 doesn't count as a st
- To customize the keychain size, ch any number + 3

Directions

ROW 1 (RS): insert hook in 2nd ch from hook, yo and pull up a loop, insert hook into 4th ch from hook, yo and pull up a loop, finish as dc, ldc across (30) [photo b]

Trim yarn, leaving an 8-inch tail. Pull your hook through and pull the yarn tight. [photo c] Fold the wristlet strip in half so the RS is facing out

Place the key chain or lobster clasp at the top of the opening. With the tapestry needle, whip stitch around both ends of the wristlet and the keychain/clasp. Weave in ends.

ch 33 with two strands of yarn [photo a]

I love cotton yarn because it's durable and has nice stitch definition. Two strands of worsted weight yarn are held double for the Luna Keychain Wristlet pattern, but you could also use a bulky or super bulky yarn. The yarn weight you choose for your crochet keychain will totally depend on what pattern you decide to follow.

| 19

Aldi Quarter Keeper

LEVEL: EASY

Materials

- Mercerized sportweight cotton yarn
- Crochet hook in size C
- Yarn needle for weaving in ends
- Keychain ring

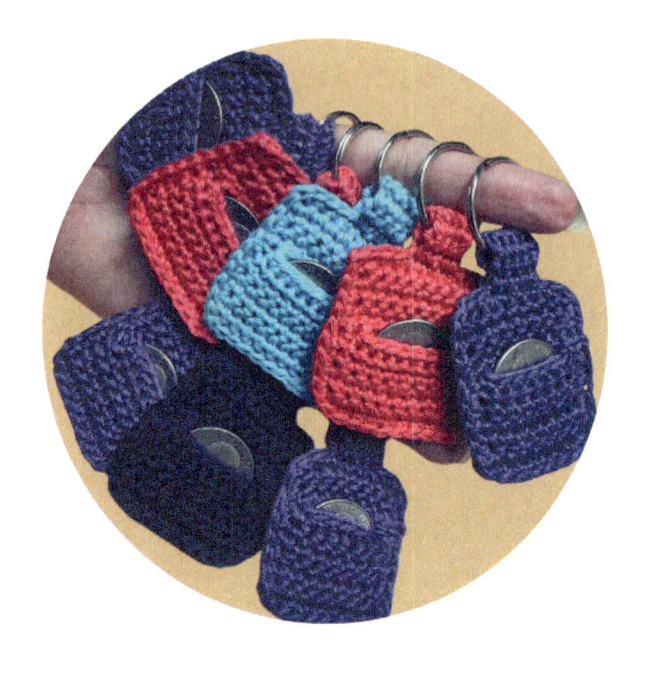

Notes

NOTE! Check the length of your chain before moving on to the rows. With some cotton yarn I need only 8 foundation single crochet stitches, while other yarns require 10. If your yarn is thicker, you may only need 19 rows as well, instead of 21.

Aldi Quarter Keeper

Directions

Using a quarter for your guide, fold ends in. Play with the placement a bit, I did about six rows for the bottom of the quarter and four rows for the top of the quarter. Use stitch markers (or not if you too live dangerously) to keep the sides lined up, and begin to single crochet through both sides around the entire square making sure to single crochet TWO in EACH corner. This helps to keep the corners from curling in. Join to beginning stitch leaving a long tail.

CREATE YOUR LOOP

At the top of the square, find your center-most four stitches in and start on your loop for the keychain ring. Attach yarn and ch-1, then sc in that same stitch and in the next three. Ch-1, turn. (4 sts) Continue with the strap for about 10 rows, then fasten off leaving a long tail and sew the end to the beginning, forming a loop for the key ring. Insert your key ring in the loop and you, my friend, are golden. Tada! It's completed!

Unicorn Earbud Holder

Materials

- Yarn: Worsted Weight / 4 Cotton Yarn / 25 yards; I used Lily Sugar n' Cream cotton yarn (colors I used are listed in the notes below)
- Crochet Hook: G/6/4.0mm (My favorite crochet hooks are the Clover Amour Hooks, I've never had an ache in my hand since switching)
- Scissors
- Yarn Needle
- Locking Stitch Markers (5)
- Key Ring (1" + or -) or Key Ring w/ a Lobster Clasp (If you do not have a key ring handy, let's brainstorm about an item we can use that we may have sitting around the house. I have an idea for one in particular.)

Special Stitches

After turning your work, do not ch, instead, insert your hook into the first st, yo, pull up a loop, yo, pull thru both loops, insert your hook between the legs of the st just made, yo, pull up a loop, yo, pull thru one loop, yo, pull thru remaining loops.

Yarn Notes:

The colors I used for my project are: White (24 yards); Pink (2 yards); Yellow (2 yards). Rainbow Hair: miscellaneous scrap of 7 colors (7" long each).

Choose ANY colors you'd like! This will look great in 1 – 3 colors. Turning chains are not included in stitch count unless noted otherwise.

Directions

Face

- Rnd 1 (RS): Using a 4.00mm crochet hook & white yarn, ch 2, work 6 sc into the 2nd ch from your hook. Join w/ a sl st to the 1st st. (6 sts)
- Rnd 2: Alt-dc in the first st, work 1 more dc in the first st w/ the alt-dc, work 2 dc in each remaining st around. Join. (12 sts)
- Approximate size: 1-1/2" diameter.
- Rnd 3: Alt-dc in the first st, work 1 more dc in the first st w/ the alt-dc, work 2 dc in each remaining st around. Join. (24 sts)
- Rnd 4: Alt-dc in the first st, work 1 more dc in the first st w/ the alt-dc, work 2 dc in each remaining st around. Join. (48 sts)
- Fasten off. Weave in ends. Use Invisible Join Technique. Continue on to Back Piece. Approximate size: 3-3/8" diameter.

Directions

Back Piece (Make 2)
- Row 1: Using a 4.00mm crochet hook & white yarn, ch 2, work 4 sc into the 2nd ch from your hook. Do not join. Turn. (4 sts)
- Row 2 (RS): Alt-dc in the first st, work 1 more dc in the first st w/ the alt-dc, work 2 dc in each remaining st around. Turn. (8 sts)
- Row 3: Alt-dc in the first st, work 2 dc in each of the next 6 sts, work 1 dc in the last st. Turn. (14 sts)
- Row 4: Alt-dc in the first st, work 1 more dc in the first st w/ the alt-dc, work 2 dc in each remaining st around. Turn. (28 sts)
- Fasten off. Weave in ends. Make one more, then continue on to Strap. Approximate size: 3-3/8" W x 1-7/8" H.

Strap
- Row 1: Using a 4.00mm crochet hook & Color B, ch 3, sc in the 2nd ch from your hook, sc in the next ch. Turn. (2 sts)
- Rows 2 – 8: Ch 1, sc in each st across. Turn. (2 sts)
- Do not fasten off. Continue on to Strap Assembly. Approximate length: 2-1/2"

Strap Assembly
- Step 1: Insert the strap through the key ring and fold it in half.
- Step 2: Ch 1, working through both layers to secure the strap on the key ring, sc in each st across. (2 sts)
- Fasten off. Weave in ends. Continue on to Eyes.

Directions

Eyes

- For the eyes I used an 18" length of black embroidery floss and a yarn needle. I chose the embroidery floss because it was easier to work with. I tried using 2 plies of the black cotton yarn, but it made a black fuzzy mess on my face.
- I first created the arch of the eye. I did this in 4 short sections to make it appear more rounded. The arch is approximately 3/4" wide *(not including the little lashes)* and 3/8" tall.
- After I finished the arch, I then made 2 small lashes on the outer corners of the eye. The little lashes are approximately 1/4" long.
- The distance between the 2 eyes is 1/4".
- After completing the eyes, continue on to Horn.

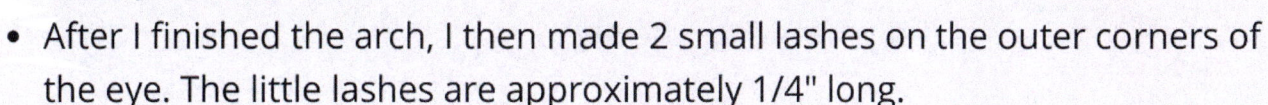

Ears (Make 2)

- Row 1 (RS): With a 4.00mm crochet hook & light pink yarn, ch 3, working into the back hump of the ch, sl st in the 2nd ch from your hook, sl st in the next ch. Turn. (2 sts). Fasten off pink yarn.
- Row 2 (RS): Join white yarn w a hdc (click here for tutorial) in the bottom of the last st from row 1, work 1 more hdc into that same st, hdc in the next st, ch 3, sl st in the 2nd ch from your hook, sc in the next ch, hdc in the next st, 2 hdc in the last st. (8 sts)
- Fasten off leaving an 8" tail of yarn for sewing.
- Continue on to Earbud Holder Assembly.

Directions

Earbud Holder Assembly

- With WS together, line up one back piece on the front motif. I add a locking SM in any stitch along the top edge of the back piece. Then, carefully lining up the stitches, place a SM in the first and last stitches of the back piece. You should have 20 stitches left between the stitch markers on the sides.

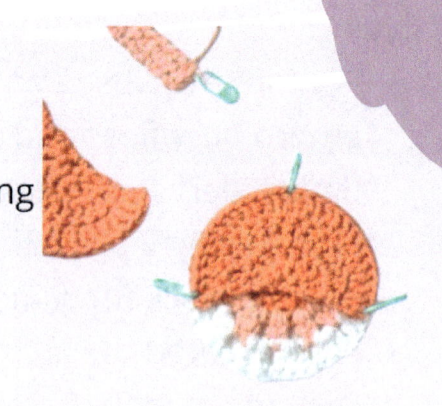

- Lay the second back piece on top of the assembly, opposite the first piece. Secure the second piece to the assembly using the SM on the side.

- To make sure that the second piece is in the correct position, you will secure it in the 4th stitch from each end.

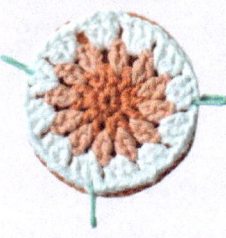

- This photo shows what your assembly should look like from the RS after securing both back pieces.

- Locate stitches #10 & #11 that were left from the first assembly photo. Insert the strap assembly between the front motif and back piece. Use stitch markers to secure the strap to stitches #10 & #11 of the holder assembly.

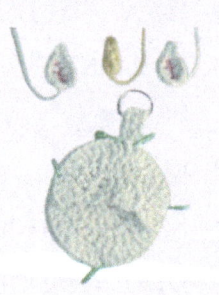

| 26

Directions

Joining

- Using a yarn needle and tail of yarn, sew the ear onto the assembled earbud holder. I sewed mine to the top loops of the stitches from the back piece. Using a yarn needle and tail of yarn, sew the horn onto the face. I centered mine on the face and sewed onto the stitches just below the slip stitch join. I had to place a couple fingers from my left hand inside the earbud holder as I did this.

Hair

Cut 7 strands of yarn approximately 7" long. I used 7 different colors. I attached the hair like I attach fringe. I attached 4 pieces to the left of the horn and 3 pieces to the right (left & right when facing you). Insert a smaller hook into the loops from the sl st join, fold the strand of hair in half and grab it with the hook, pull it thru the stitch. Insert the cut ends of the yarn through the loop you just made and pull to tighten.

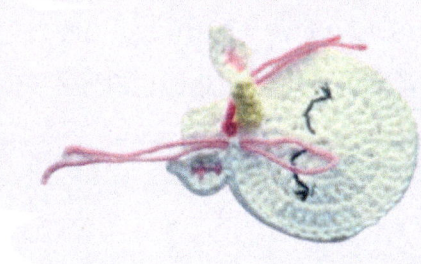

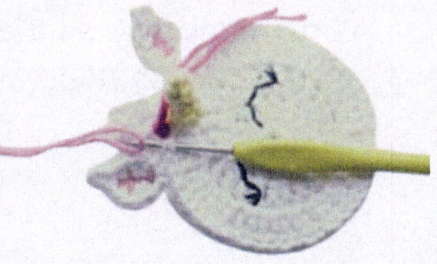

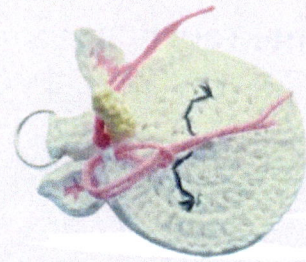

Directions

Hair
Attach the remaining strands of hair.

To make it easier to manipulate, trim the hair to around eye level. Then begin separating the plies of yarn to give it a fuller and slightly wavy look. After you've separated all of the plies of yarn, trim the hair one last time to the length you prefer. Mine ended up being around 1" long.

Final Touch: Use a make-up brush and add a little blush to the cheeks. See photo above.Final Touch: Use a make-up brush and add a little blush to the cheeks.

Santa lip balm holder

Materials

- Yarn in 4 colors - Ricorumi DK 100% cotton, 25 g (57.5 m). Red, Black, Yellow and White (optional white velvet yarn)
- Crochet hook size E (3.5 mm).
- A darning needle
- Stitch markers
- A pair of scissors
- Metal spring hook or keyring

Gauge

13 stitches and 11 rows = 5 cm in single crochet

Size

This lip balm holder measures approx. 4.13 " (10.5 cm) in height to the top of the hat.

Yardage

Weight: 6 grams. Yardage: Approximately 14m (15.3 yards)

Pattern notes

- You can make the pattern larger or smaller by changing the type of yarn and/or hook size. Depending on the size of your lip balm, lipstick or lip gloss, you might want to add a few rounds to increase height.
- Numbers at the end of each round (in brackets) indicate the number of final stitches in that round.
- Please ensure that your lip balm is the size of the bottom of the holder after round 2.
- Insert your lip balm, lipstick or lip gloss into the holder when you get to almost the end to see if you need to add a few rounds to adjust height.
- We'll be working in the round, so a stitch marker is advised.
- Please note that I use US crochet terms.

Directions

Body

- Round 1: With Red yarn, work 6 sc into a MC. If you don't know how to crochet a MC, start with Ch 2, then crochet 6 sc into the second chain from the hook (6).
- Pull the tail end to close the circle. We will be working in continuous rounds so insert a stitch marker into the first st of each upcoming round.

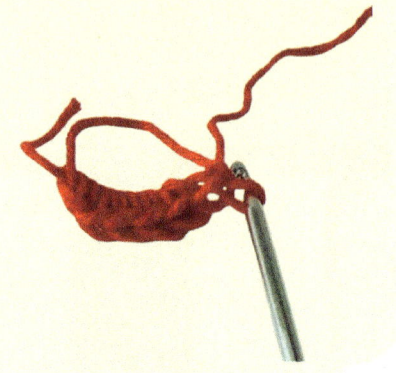

Directions

Body

- Round 2: 2 sc into each stitch around (12).

Note: Place your lip-balm on this circle and check that it fits nicely inside the circle.

- Rounds 3-9: sc into each stitch around (12). [7 rounds]

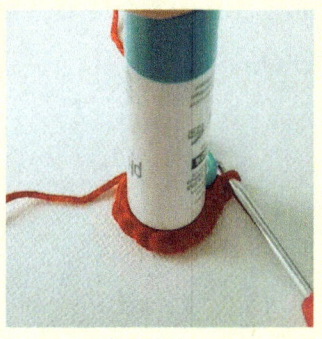

- Round 10: Drop red yarn, join black yarn, sc into each stitch around (12).

Note: Learn how to join colors neatly. You do not need to cut the red yarn since you'll be using it again after 2 rounds.

- Round 11: Sc into each st around (12). Leaving a 4" tail, cut your black yarn.
- Round 12-14: Join red yarn, sc into each stitch around (12). [3 rounds]

Directions

Hanger

- Chain 30. Attach the end to the opposite side of the top of the chapstick holder with a sl st, 6 sts apart.
- Leaving a 4" tail, cut your yarn and fasten off.
- Weave in end and secure the hanger with a couple of stitches from the inside. cut off excess.

Buckle

- Cut a 10" piece of yellow yarn and thread through your darning needle.
- Stitch a rectangle on the front black section of Santa's body in the shape of a buckle (2 short stitches on the sides and 2 longer sts on the top & bottom about 4 sts across).
- Tie a double knot with the two ends from the inside of the lip balm holder to secure. Cut off excess.

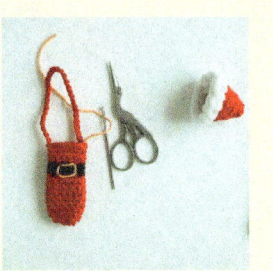

| 32

Directions

Hat

- Round 1: With red yarn, start off with a MC, then work 4 sc into the MC. Pull the tail and loosely close the MC (4). *Don't close it too tight because we'll be pulling the hanger through this little hole in the end.*

Note: We'll be working in continuous rounds, so best to use a stitch marker to mark the first st of each round.

- Round 2: 2 sc into the first st, sc into the next 3 sts (5).
- Round 3: 2 sc into the first st, sc into the next 4 sts (6).
- Round 4: 2 sc into the first st, sc into the next 5 sts (7).

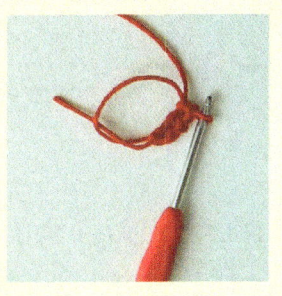

- Round 5: 2 sc into the first st, sc into the next 6 sts (8).
- Round 6: 2 sc into the first st, sc into the next 7 sts (9).
- Round 7: 2 sc into the first st, sc into the next 8 sts (10).
- Round 8:.2 sc into the first st, sc into the next 9 sts (11).
- Round 9: 2 sc into the first st, sc into the next 10 sts (12). Leave a 4" tail, cut yarn.

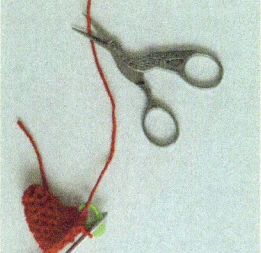

Directions

Hat

- Round 10: Join white yarn, sc into each st around (12). You can use any type of yarn here... the same cotton DK or a more fluffy yarn. I used velvet yarn for this Santa hat.
- Leave a 4" tail, cut your yarn and fo by joining the last st to the first st of this round to smooth out the brim of the hat. Weave in ends.

Attach Keyring

- Insert your hook inwards into the top of the hat and catch the chain that's attached to the body to pull it through the top of the hat.
- Attach the metal keyring to the end of your long red chain.
- And there you have it! Your very own Santa lip-balm holder keychain that you can keep for yourself or gift to someone special this Christmas.

| 34

Animal keychain patterns

Cat Keychain

LEVEL: EASY

Materials

- Yarn: Orange or yellow, white
- Hook: 2.5mm
- Cotton
- Eyes: 5mm

Directions

Start with orange (or yellow) yarn,
R1: MR 6sc
R2: inc*6R3: (inc, sc)*6
R4: (2sc, inc)*6
R5: (3sc, inc)*6 = 30
R6: 14sc, (white sc), 15sc = 30
R7: 13sc, (white 3sc), 14sc = 30
R8: 12sc, (white 5sc), 13sc = 30

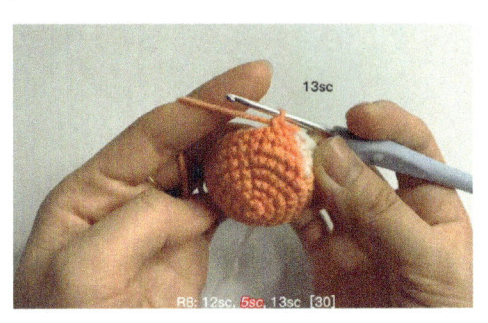

Directions

R9: white 30sc = 30
R10: (white 3sc, dec)*6 = 24
R11: (white 2sc, dec)*6 = 18
R12: (white sc, dec)*6 = 12
R13: (white 12sc) = 12
Ear: 3ch, slst
Eyes: R7

Ear: 3ch, slst

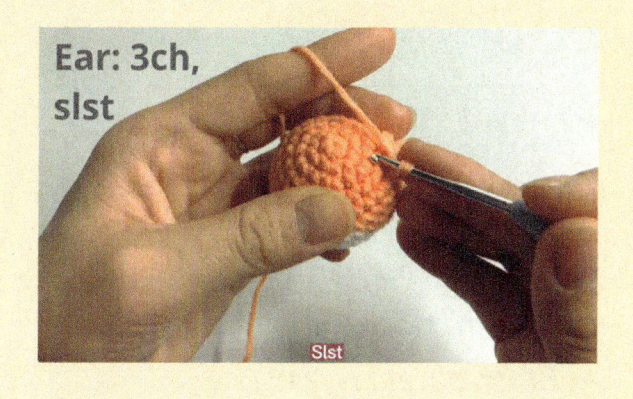

Put eyes between round 7 and 8

Making mouth and whiskers

Create three lines in the cat's forehead

Koala Keychain

`LEVEL: EASY`

Materials

- Paintbox Yarns Cotton DK in Stormy Grey and Paper White
- 2.5mm hook
- 6mm safety eyes
- Polyester fiberfill
- A small piece of black felt
- Black embroidery floss
- Keychain
- Yarn needle, stitch marker, scissors

Notes:

The pattern is written using US terminology and measures approximately 2.5" (6.5cm) x 2" (5cm).

Pieces are worked in a continuous spiral starting with a magic ring unless otherwise specified. Mark the first stitch of each round with a removable stitch marker.

Gauge is not important in this pattern. Use a hook size to match your chosen yarn. Make sure that your stitches are tight enough to prevent stuffing showing through and adjust hook size if necessary.

Directions

HEAD

R1: 6 sc in magic ring (6)
R2: [Inc] x6 (12)
R3: [Sc, inc] x6 (18)
R4: Sc, inc, [2 sc, inc] x5, sc (24)
R5: [3 sc, inc] x6 (30)
R6: 2 sc, inc, [4 sc, inc] x5, 2 sc (36)
R7: FLO sc around (36)
R8: Sc around (36)
R9: FLO 2 sc, invdec, [4 sc, invdec] x5, 2 sc (30)
R10: [3 sc, invdec] x6 (24)
R11: Sc, invdec, [2 sc, invdec] x5, sc (18)

Insert the safety eyes between rounds 4 and 5, approximately 1 stitch up from the center and with 5 stitches in between.

Trim stems off the back of the eyes and stuff lightly.

R12: [Sc, invdec] x6 (12)
R13: [Invdec] x6 (6). Fasten off and weave in end.

EARS (make 2, white)

R1: 4 sc in magic ring (4)
R2: Ch 1, turn. Inc in each st (8)
R3: Ch 1, turn. Sc, inc (12)
Fasten off and weave in ends.
Make 2, grey

R1: 4 sc in magic ring (4)
R2: Ch 1, turn. Inc in each st (8)
R3: Ch 1, turn. Sc inc (12)
R4: Ch 1, turn. Place the white piece against the grey piece with right sides facing out.
Sc in each st on both pieces to join together (12)

Fasten off, leaving a long tail for sewing. Repeat for the 2nd ear.

ASSEMBLY

Sew ears to the top of the head approximately 5 stitches apart. Cut a small oval of felt for the nose and glue or felt in place centered between the eyes. Embroider a mouth if desired. Attach a keychain to the top.

Fish keychain

Materials

- Yarn: 330m/100g in two colors plus black, I had YarnArt Jeans;
- Stuffing;
- 2,5 mm hook;
- Needle;
- Scissors.

Notes:

- Crochet in continuous rounds, unless the signs indicate otherwise. In brackets there is the total number of stitches in a given row.

Directions

Body (Blue)
R1) mr 6sc (6)
R2) (sc, inc)x3 (9)
R3) 9sc (9)
R4) (2sc, inc)x3 (12)
R5) (sc, inc)x6 (18)
R6) 18sc (18)
R7) (2sc, inc)x6 (24) Change color and continue with yellow.
R8) 24sc, sl (24) Change color and continue with blue.
R9) (3sc, inc)x6, sl (30) Change color and continue with yellow.
R8) 30sc, sl (30) Change color and continue with blue.
R9) (4sc, inc)x6 (36)
R10-16) 36sc (36)

| 40

Directions

Body:

Last round ends with slip stitch.
Next: 5 chain and from the second ch from hook: 4sl. Put the piece in half and connect the two edges with sc. After about 2/3 of connecting fill the body with stuffing and make sc to the end of row. Then make again 5 chain and from the second ch from hook: 4sl. Cut and hide the thread.

TAIL: Yellow

R1) Find the three central stitches at the back of the fish. Make 3 sc, catching only the front thread, turn the work. Make 3 sc at the same stitches as before, grabbing the remaining thread (6)
R2) 6inc (12) Change color and continue with blue.
R3) 12sc (12)
R4) (sc, inc)x6 (18) Don't fill with stuffing. Fold out and join sides with sc. Cut and hide the thread.

Directions

FINS Yellow

R1) In the middle of 14 rounds in one stitch make: 3ch, 5dc, ch, and turn work.

R2) 6sc Cut and hide the thread. Make another fin at the other side.

Sew eyes between 3 and 4 rounds, place keychain ring and your fish is done

Rabbit Keychain

LEVEL: EASY

Materials

- Yarn: Jeans art 03, 23, 69.
- Hook: Size 2.3 mm
- Two 6mm safety eyes

Directions

HEAD

Rnd 1: 6 sc in the magic ring (6)
Rnd 2: 6 inc (12)
Rnd 3: (1 sc, inc)*6 (18)
Rnd 4: (inc, 2 sc)*6 (24)
Rnd 5: (3 sc, inc)*6 (30)
Rnd 6: 1 sc, inc, (4 sc, inc)*5, 3 sc (36)
Rnd 7: 36 sc (36)
Rnd 8: (5 sc, inc)*6 (42)
Rnd 9-13: 42 sc (42)
Rnd14: (5 sc, dec)*6 (36)
Rnd 15: 36 sc (36)
Rnd 16: 2 sc, dec, (4 sc, dec)*5, 2 sc (30)

Directions

HEAD

Rnd 17: (3 sc, dec)*6 (24)

Rnd 18: 1 sc, dec, (2 sc, dec)*5, 1sc (18)

Rnd 19: (1 sc, dec)*6 (12)

Fasten off the yarn. Stuff the head. Put in the eyes between rows 11-12, leaving 6 stitches space between them.

EAR

Rnd 1: 6 sc in the magic ring (6)

Rnd 2: (1sc, inc)*3 (9)

Rnd 3: (inc, 2 sc)*3 (12)

Rnd 4: (1 sc, inc)*6 (18)

Rnd 5-8: 18 sc (18)

Rnd 9: (4 sc, dec)*3 (15)

Rnd 10: 15 sc (15)

Rnd 11: (3 sc, dec)*3 (12)

Rnd 12: (2 sc, dec)*3 (9)

Fastten off the yarn, leaving a long tail for sewing. Do not stuff.

Fold the top of the ear, sew the 2 opposed stitches.

ARM

Rnd 1: 6 sc in the magic ring (6)

Rnd 2: (1 sc, inc)*3 (9)

Rnd 3-8: 9 sc (9)

Slst and fasten off the yarn, leaving a long tail for sewing. Do not stuff.

Fold the top of the arm, sew the 2 opposed stitches.

Directions

LEG

Rnd 1: 6 sc in the magic ring (6)

Rnd 2: 6 inc (12)

Rnd 3: (1 sc, inc)*6 (18)

Rnd 4-5: 18 sc (18).

CARROT

Rnd 1: 6 sc in the magic ring (6)

Rnd 2: 6 inc (12)

Rnd 3: 12 sc (12)

Rnd 4: (3 sc, inc)*3 (15)

Rnd 5: 15 sc (15)

Rnd 6: (4 sc, inc)*3 (18)

Rnd 7: 18 sc (18)

Rnd 6: 4 sc, 5 dec, 4 sc (13)

Rnd 7: 5 sc, 2 dec, 4 sc (11)

Rnd 8-10: 11 sc (11)

Slst and fasten off the yarn, leaving a long tail for sewing. Stuff the leg

Rnd 8: (5 sc, inc)*3 (21)

Rnd 9-11: 21 sc (21)

Rnd 12: (5 sc, dec)*3 (18)

Stuff the carrot.

Rnd 13: (1 sc, dec)*6 (12)

Rnd 14: 6 dec, slst. (6)

LEAVES

(make 8 ch, start in the second ch from the hook : 7 slst)*3

Directions

TAIL

Rnd 1: 6 sc in the magic ring (6)

Rnd 2: 6 inc (12)

Rnd 3: (3 sc, inc)*3 (15)

Rnd 4: (3 sc, dec)*3 (12)

Slst and fasten off the yarn, leaving a long tail for sewing. Stuff the tail. Then assemle and enjoy your cute rabbit keychain!

Fruits and food keychain patterns

Mandarin Keychain

Materials

- 4-ply cotton blend yarn in orange, green, yellow and white (recommend Alize Cotton Gold)
- 2.00mm crochet hook Stitch marker.
- Fiberfill.
- Yarn needle. Scissors. Glue gun. Keychain ring

Notes:

- This pattern is written using and is worked in rounds, US terms do not join at the end of the round unless stated otherwise.
- Using a similar yarn and hook size as mine, the mandarin will be approx. 4 cm.

Directions

Flower: With yellow,

- R1: 5sc in MC (5)
- Change to white.
- R2: [ch6, slst on 2nd ch from hook. In next chains: 1sc, 1dc, 1dc, 1hdc, slst in BLO of the next yellow sc]. Repeat 5 times to get 5 petals.

Fasten off and weave in ends. With a glue gun, glue the flower on the stem part of the leaf. Attach a keychain to the top at the end!

Directions

Mandarin: With orange,
- R1: 7sc in MC (7)
- R2: 7inc (14)
- R3: 1sc, 1inc (21)
- R4: 2sc, 1inc (28)
- R5: sc all around (28)
- R6: 3sc, 1inc (35)
- R7-R10: sc all around (35) -4 rows
- R11: 3sc, 1dec (28)
- R12: 2sc, 1dec (21
- Stuff with fiberfill.
- R13: 1sc, 1dec (14)
- R14: 7dec (7)
- Fasten off. Using a yarn needle, sew the hole close and weave in end.

Leaf and stem:
- With green, leave tail at the beginning to sew on the mandarin later.
- Ch7, sc on 2nd ch from hook, sc in next 4ch.
- In last ch: (1sc, 1slst).
- DO NOT FASTEN OFF.
- Proceed to crochet the leaf:
- ch8, slst on 2nd ch from hook. In the next chains:
- 1sc, 1hdc, 1dc, 1dc, 1tc, 2dc in last ch.
- On the other side of the
- foundation chain: 2dc in one ch, 1tc,
- 1dc, 1dc, 1hdc, 1sc, 1slst.
- Fasten off and weave in the end.
- Using the beginning tail, sew the leaf and stem on top of the mandarin.

Avocado Keychain

LEVEL: EASY

Materials

- 3.5mm hook
- Bernat Super Value in Lush
- Loops & Threads Impeccable in Grass;
- Bernat Premium in Evergreen;
- Bernat Premium in Chocolate Tweed;
- Light weight yarn in pink for the cheeks;
- Black crochet thread for mouth
- 8mm Safety Eyes;
- Keyring;
- Stuffing;
- Tapestry needle

Directions

Ch 1 and turn at the end of each row

- Front Body (make 1 panel) starting in Grass:
- Row 1: Ch 8, sc across (7 sts)
- Row 2: Inc, sc 5, inc (9 sts)

Directions

- Row 3: Inc, sc 7, inc (11 sts)
- Rows 4-6: Sc across (11 sts)
- Row 7: Dec, sc 7, dec (9 sts)
- Rows 8-9: Sc across (9 sts)
- Row 10: Dec, sc 5, dec (7 sts)
- Rows 11-12: Sc across (7 sts)
- Row 13: Dec, sc 3, dec (5 sts)
- Row 14: Dec, hdc, dec (3 sts)
- Do not tie off yet. Join Lush coloured yarn and chain 1, then single crochet around the entire panel in Lush. You should have 37 sts around.

Back Body (make 1 panel) in Evergreen:

Repeat rows 1-14 above for the back body panel in Evergreen. Do not tie off. Ch 1 and single crochet around the entire panel in Evergreen (37 sts).

Pit (make 1) in Chocolate Tweed:

Rnd 1: MR 7 sc (7 sts)

Rnd 2: Inc around (14 sts)

Rnds 3-4: Sc 4, hdc, dc, hdc, sc 4, hdc, dc, hdc (14 sts).

Slst to next st and tie off.

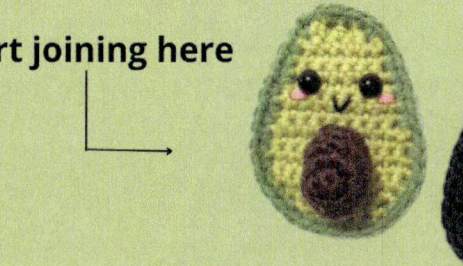

Start joining here

Directions

- Assembly:

Step 1: Pit, Eyes, Mouth, and Cheeks

- First, we need to attach our pit and all of our facial features to the front panel.
- With a length of Chocolate Tweed yarn about 30cm/12" long, stitch the pit onto the centre of the front panel. Stuff lightly after you've stitched it about three-quarters of the way around, like so:
- Next, insert 8mm safety eyes and then stitch on the cheeks below each eye using pink yarn.
- Stitch on the mouth using black crochet thread.

Step 2: Body

Place the two body panels together, matching up all sides.

Make sure the front of your Avocado is facing you as you crochet around the outside of the piece. ** Starting on the left side, begin attaching the panels together by chaining one and single crocheting around the outside of the panels in **Evergreen. Crochet all the way down and around the Avocado and up the opposite side. Stop here and pull up a long loop. Stuff your Avocado.

Now, picking up where you left off, continue single crocheting around the outside. Top up stuffing as you go, if necessary.

Close with a slst to first st. Tie off. With your tapestry needle, poke the yarn tail back inside the piece.

Attach a key ring at the top and you're done!

Lemon Keychain

LEVEL: EASY

Materials

- Thin-weight yarn of your choice (yellow, green, pink).
- Size 1,25 mm Crochet Hook.
- Scissors.
- Thread (black).
- Beads, 4 mm (black).
- Keychain Cord.
- Transparent plastic Crystal Anti Dust Cap Plug Earphone Jack 3.5mm.
- Hand Sewing Needles.
- Filling Material for toys.

Directions

1 step. Make 2 ch, in second ch from the hook make 6 sc, 1 sl st in the first sc (top of sc). (6)

Directions

2 step. Make 1 ch, 1 sc in each of next 6 loops. At the end of the row make 1 sl st in the first sc. (6)

3 step. Make 1 ch, 2 sc in each of next loops, at the end of the row make 1 sl st in the first sc. (12)

4 step. Make 1 ch, 1 sc in each of next loops, at the end of the row make 1 sl st in the first sc. (12)

5 step. Make 1 ch, repeat cluster (2 sc, 1 sc) 6 times yet. At the end of the row make 1 sl st in the first sc. (18) In next row make 1 ch, repeat cluster (1 sc*2, 2 sc) 6 times yet. At the end of the row make 1 sl st n the first sc. (24)

Directions

6 step. Make 1 ch, repeat cluster (2 sc, 1 sc*3) 6 times yet. At the end of the row make 1 sl st in the first sc. (30)

7 step. In each of next 9 rows make 1 ch, 1 sc in each of next loop, 1 sl st in the first sc. (30)

8 step. Cut a small yellow thread and fold it in half 2 times. Then make a loop. Insert the hook into the top of the lemon, grab the crochet thread and drag it out. Fix in the loop the carabiner of the lace for the keychain-pendant.

9 step. Sew the black beads (eyes), embroider a mouth and blush on the cheeks.

10 step. Attach the anti dust cap to the cord.

Directions

11 step. Go back to the crocheting of the lemon. Make 1 ch, (2 sc tog, 1 ch*3) - repeat it 6 times yet, at the end of the row make 1 sl st in the first sc. (24)

12 step. Make 1 ch, (1 sc*2, 2 sc tog) - repeat it around, at the end make 1 sl st in the first sc. (18)

13 step. Fill the lemon with polyester toy filling. For the next rows, add a little filler each time.

14 step. Make 1 ch, (1 sc, 2 sc tog) - repeat it around, at the end make 1 sl st in the first sc. (12)

15 step. Make 1 ch, (2 sc tog) - repeat it around, at the end make 1 sl st in the first sc. (6)

16 step. Make 1 ch, 1 sc*6, 1 sl st in the first sc. (6)

17 step. Repeat the previous row. (6)

18 step. Connect together all tops of sc. Use yarn tail to weave in and out of the remaining stitches, pull tight to close the gap, knot off and hide yarn tail inside the body.

| 56

Directions

19 step. Begin to crochet a leaf. Take a green yarn. Make 15 ch.

20 step. Skip first ch, in next loops make sequence - 1 sc, 1 hdc, 1 dc*2, 1 tr*5, 1 dc*2, 1 hdc, 1 sc, 1 sl st.

21 step. Make 1 ch, on another side of chain space make sequence - 1 sc, 1 hdc, 1 dc*2, 1 tr*5, 1 dc*2, 1 hdc, 1 sc 1 sl st in the top of sc. Finish, leaving long tail.

22 step. Crochet the second leaf. In the second leaf leave a short thread at the end of the work and hide it on the wrong side. Sew both leaves to the top of the lemon.

Apple Keychain

LEVEL: EASY

Materials

- In order to create the mini apple you will use Cotton 8/4 and a 2mm crochet hook, if you want to create the Keychain size you might want to use Cotton 8/8.

For the mini apple I used:

- 2 mm crochet hook
- Cotton Kings 8/4 n. 10 (Red) – less than 5gr.
- Cotton Kings 8/4 n. 41 (Spring Green) – less than 1gr.
- Rainbow Cotton 8/4 n. 008 (Dark Brown) – less than 1gr.

For the keychain apple I used:

- 3.5 mm crochet hook
- Cotton We Love Yarn 8/8 n. 16 (Red) – less than 10gr.
- Rainbow Cotton 8/8 n. 99 (Malachite Green) – less than 1gr.
- Rainbow Cotton 8/8 n. 05 (Grey Brown) – less than 1gr.

Notes:

I bought the yarn at Hobbii.
For both projects you will need:
- stitch marker
- stuffing
- darning needle

I bought the yarn at Hobbii.

Directions

STALK

- **START**

With Dark Brown, leave a long initial tails (about 7/8cm) and then do a slip knot and CH 5.

- **ROUND 1**

Starting from 2nd CH from the hook, SS 4. (4)
Leave a long tail (about 7/8cm) and fasten off.

LEAF

- **START**

With Spring Green, leave a long initial tails (about 7/8cm), do a slip knot and then CH 6.

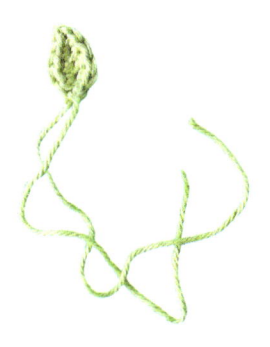

- **ROUND 1**

Starting from 2nd CH from hook, SS 1, SC 1, HDC 2, 3 SS in the last CH.
Now we will crochet in the other side of the chain: HDC 2, SC 1, SS 1, fasten off. (11)
With the darning needle weave the end through the leaf so that the tails (initial tail and end tail) will be together.

APPLE

ROUND 1 (With Red) SC 6 in a magic ring. (6)
ROUND 2 [SC 2, INC] x 2 times. (8)
ROUND 3 [SC 1, INC] x 4 times. (12)
ROUND 4 [SC 1, INC] x 6 times. (18)

Directions

APPLE

- **ROUND 5**

[SC 2, INC] x 6 times. (24)

Now it's the moment to add the stalk and the leaf to the top of the apple.

Using a darning needle, we will insert the threads of the stalk and we insert them in the middle of the MC that we did at the beginning. We will do the same then with the leaf, see PIC n. 1.

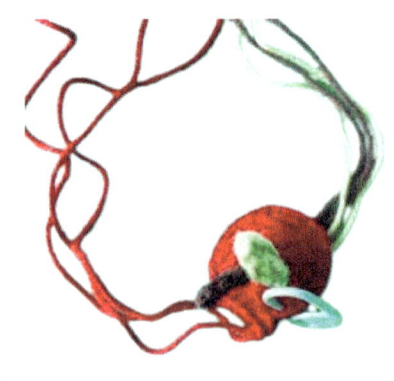

Now we turn the work upside down and we press the top up to the wrong side, so we will see better the threads we just put through the MC, see PIC n. 2.

We will make a doulbe knot for each pair of thread and we cut the extra thread, see PIC n. 3.

Now we press the work back to the right side and we continue with the pattern.

ROUND 6-9 (4 Rounds) SC 24 (24)

ROUND 10 [SC 2, DEC] x 6 times (18)

ROUND 11 [SC 1, DEC] x 6 times (12)

Fill the apple with stuffing, trying to stuff less on the top part (where you attached the stem and the leaf – round 1 and 2)

Round 1 and 2 will be pressed inside the apple, instructions after Round 12.

Directions

APPLE

- **ROUND 12**

DEC all around (6)

Cut a long tail (about 15cm), close the apple passing the thread in the front loop of the last 6SC and pull tight.

If, instead, you will prefer a normal loop, follow the instructions below.

You will insert the hook in the middle of the stitches we just closed (PIC n. 4) and we take the needle out from the opposite side, close to the centre of the top (PIC N. 5) and then we will insert the needle in the centre of the original MC (PIC n. 6), we pull tight in order to low stem and leaf inside the apple (PIC n. 7). Now weave the end and cut the thread.

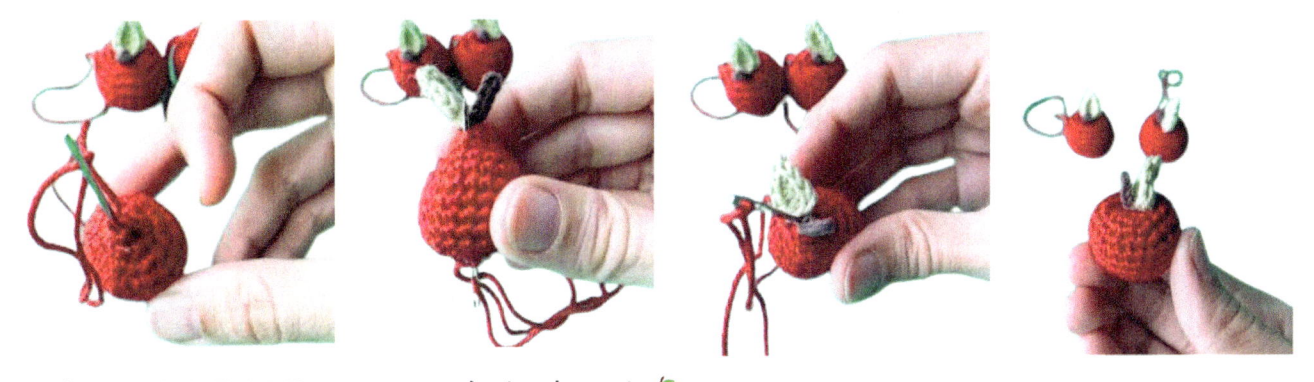

And HERE WE ARE: your apple is done! 🍎

Strawberry keychain

LEVEL: EASY

Materials

- 3.0 mm (C USA, 11 UK) Crochet Hook
- DK (3, Light) Weight Yarn
- One Stitch Marker (to work in the round)
- Poly-Fil or Cotton Stuffing
- White Embroidery Floss
- Tapestry Needle
- Embroidery Needle

Yarns

I used Hobbii Rainbow Cotton 8/6 (50 g, 115 yds / 105 m) in the following colors:
- A – Light Coral (050)
- B – Dusty Light Green (075)

Specials stiches

Increase (Inc) One increase consists of two sts worked in the same indicated st.
Invisible Decrease (Inv Dec). Magic Circle (MC)

Patterns notes:

- If the pattern says "sc 2", it means that you have to crochet 1 sc into each of the next 2 sts.
- (...) – Repeat the instruction within brackets for the indicated number of times.
- The stitch count is indicated within brackets at the end of each line of instructions.

LARGE STRAWBERRY (Work in the round)

With **A**, make an MC.

Round 1. Sc 6 in MC. (*6 sts*)
Round 2. (Sc 2, sc inc 1**) twice**. (*8 sts*)
Round 3. (Sc 1, sc inc 1**) 4** times. (*12 sts*)
Round 4. (Sc 5, sc inc 1**) twice**. (*14 sts*)
Round 5. Sc 3, sc inc 1, sc 6, sc inc 1, sc 3. (*16 sts*)
Round 6. (Sc 7, sc inc 1**) twice**. (*18 sts*)
Round 7. Sc 4, sc inc 1, sc 8, sc inc 1, sc 4. (*20 sts*)
Round 8. (Sc inc 1, sc 3**) 5** times. (*25 sts*)
Round 9-11. Sc all around. (*25 sts*)
Round 12. (Sc 3, inv dec 1**) 5** times. (*20 sts*)
Round 13. Sc 1, sc inv dec 1, **(**sc 2, inv dec 1**) 4** times, sc 1. (*15 sts*)
Start filling up your strawberry.
Round 14. (Inv dec 1, sc 1**) 5** times. (*10 sts*)
Fasten off and close the last 10 sts together by sewing through the front loops. Weave in all your ends.

Directions

STEM

With B, ch 3.
Row 1. Sl st 2 starting from the second ch from hook. (2 sts)
Fasten off leaving a long tail for sewing.

LARGE LEAVES

With B, make an MC.
Round 1. Ch 1 (does not count as a st), sc 6 in MC, sl st in first st to join. (6 sts)
Round 2. (Ch 3, sl st in second ch from hook, sc 1, sl st 1 in next st on round 1) 6 times. (6 leaves)
Fasten off leaving a long tail for sewing.

SMALL STRAWBERRY

(Work in the round)
With A, make a MC.
Round 1. Sc 6 in MC. (6 sts)
Round 2. (Sc 2, sc inc 1) twice. (8 sts)
Round 3. (Sc 1, sc inc 1) 4 times. (12 sts)
Round 4. (Sc 5, sc inc 1) twice. (14 sts)
Round 5. Sc 3, sc inc 1, sc 6, sc inc 1, sc 3. (16 sts)
Round 6. (Sc inc 1, sc 3) 4 times. (20 sts)
Round 7-8. Sc around. (20 sts)
Round 9. (Sc 2, inv dec 1) 5 times. (15 sts)
Start filling up your strawberry.
Round 10. (Sc 1, inv dec 1) 5 times. (10 sts)
Fasten off and close the last 10 sts together by sewing through the front loops.
Weave in all your ends.

STEM

With B, ch 3.
Row 1. Sl st 2 starting from second ch from hook. (2 sts)
Fasten off leaving a long tail for sewing.

Directions

SMALL LEAVES

With B, make a MC.

Round 1. Ch 1 (does not count as a st), sc 6 in MC, sl st in first st to join. (6 sts)

Round 2. (Ch 3, sl st in second ch from hook, sc 1, sl st 1 in next st on round 1) 6 times. (6 leaves)

Fasten off leaving a long tail for sewing.

ASSEMBLY – BOTH LARGE AND SMALL STRAWBERRY

With white embroidery floss and embroidery needle, embroider the strawberry seeds.

Sew the stem in the center of the leaves, and then, attach the leaves on top of the strawberry.

Weave in all your ends.

Mini pumpkin keychain

Materials
- Orange, Brown, and green yarn. I suggest Hobby Lobby's "I love this cotton!" or cotton of any brand. However, you can use any yarn you prefer. Just be aware that this may change the size of your pumpkin.
- A key chain of any sort.
- 3.5 mm (E) crochet hook.
- Scissors and needle.

Directions
Pumpkin:
Rnd 1: Sc 6 in MR (6)
Rnd 2: Inc Around (12)
Rnd 3: (Sc 1, Inc) repeat around (18)
Rnd 4: (Sc 2, Inc) repeat around (24) Rnd 5-10: Sc around. (24)

Directions

Pumpkin:

Rnd 5-10: Sc around. (24)

Rnd 11: (Dec, Sc 1) Repeat around.

Rnd 12: Dec around.

F/O Leave a long tail. Sew the hole closed Use the tail to wrap around the pumpkin very tightly to create the bulges. Each time you will need to use your needle to go in through the bottom and out the top.

Stem:

Rnd 1: Sc 6 in MR (6)

Rnd 2: Sc around in BLO (6)

Rnd 3: Sc around. (6) Leave a long tail. Sew to top of the pumpkin.

Leaf:

1. Ch 7.

2. Continuing down the side, DC INC 1. DC INC 1. DC. HDC. SC. SS. 3. Going back towards the bottom: SC. HDC. DC INC 1. DC INC 1.

Sew the leaf to the side of the stem. Attach the keychain ring to the top of the stem.

Pizza Keychain

LEVEL: EASY

Materials

- 3.0 mm (C USA, 11 UK) Crochet Hook
- DK (3, Medium) Weight Yarn
- One Stitch Marker (to work in the round)
- Tapestry Needle

Yarns & colors

For my Pizza Slice Amigurumi, I used Paintbox Yarns Cotton DK in the following colors:

- A – Mustard Yellow (424)
- B – Champagne White (403)
- C – Rose Red (414)
- D – Grass Green (430)

Size

Each slice measures 2" (5 cm) in length by 2" (5 cm) in width in the largest point.

Notes

- If the pattern says "sc 2", it means that you have to crochet 1 sc into each of the next 2 sts.
- (...) – Repeat the instruction within brackets for the indicated number of times.
- The stitch count is indicated within brackets at the end of each line of instructions.
- The pizza slice pattern is worked in the round. This means that you do not join with a sl st. Instead, you start crocheting the next round directly in the first st of the previous round.
- The mozzarella decoration is worked in rows.

Directions

PIZZA SLICE

(Work in the round)

With A, make a MC.

Round 1. Sc 6 in MC (6 sts)

Round 2. (Sc inc 1, sc 2) twice. (8 sts)

Round 3. Sc 8.

Round 4. (Sc inc 1, sc 3) twice. (10 sts)

Round 5. (Sc inc 1, sc 4) twice. (12 sts)

Round 6. (Sc inc 1, sc 5) twice. (14 sts)

Round 7. (Sc inc 1, sc 6) twice. (16 sts)

Round 8. (Sc inc 1, sc 7) twice. (18 sts)

Round 9. (Sc inc 1, sc 8) twice. (20 sts)

Round 10. (Sc inc 1, sc 9) twice. (22 sts)

Round 11. (Sc inc 1, sc 10) twice. (24 sts)

Round 12. Sc 24.

Round 13. (Sc inc 1, sc 11) twice. (26 sts)

Round 14-15. Sc 26.

Directions

Crust

Row 16. Sl st 1, ch 1, turn. Sc 13.

Row 17-20. Ch 1, turn. Sc 13.

Fasten off leaving a long tail for sewing.

Mozzarella & Tomato

With **B**, ch 2. **Row 1 (WS).** Sc 2 in the first-made ch. (2 sts)

Row 2 (RS). Ch 1 (does not count as a st here and in the rest of the pattern), turn. Sc inc 2. (4 sts)

Row 3. Ch 1, turn. Sc 4.

Row 4. Ch 1, turn. Sc 1, sc inc 2, sc 1. (6 sts)

Row 5. Ch 1, turn. Sc 6.

Row 6. Ch 1, turn. Sc 2, sc inc 2, sc 2. (8 sts)

Row 7. Ch 1, turn. Sc 8.

Row 8. Ch 1, turn. Sc 3, sc inc 2, sc 3. (10 sts)

Row 9. Ch 1, turn. Sc 10.

Row 10 (RS). Ch 1, turn. Sc 1, hdc 1, sc 1, sl st 3, sc 1, dc 2, hdc 1. (10 sts)

Fasten off leaving a long tail for sewing.

RS facing, join C in the BLO of the first st of row 10.

Row 11. [BLO sc 1, BLO sl st 1], BLO sl st 6, BLO sc 2, [BLO sc 3], sl st on the side of the last hdc of row 10. (14 sts)

Fasten off leaving a long tail for sewing.

Directions

BASIL LEAVES

With D, ch 4.

Row 1. Sc 1 in the second ch from hook, hdc inc 1, sl st 1. Ch 3, sc inc 1 in the second ch from hook, sl st 1, sl st back into the first-made ch.

Fasten off leaving a long tail for sewing.

PIZZA SLICE ASSEMBLY

Flatten the pizza slice by squeezing the open half of round 15 onto the pizza crust.

Sew the Mozzarella & Tomato on the top half of the pizza slice. Then, attach the basil leaves.

Roll the crust of the pizza and sew it in place. First, sew the last row of the crust with row 18. Them, roll the crust once more and sew it across both layers of round 15.

Fasten off and weave in all your ends.

WELL DONE, YOUR CROCHET **PIZZA SLICE KEYCHAIN** IS READY!

Taco Keychain

LEVEL: EASY

Materials

- Worsted weight yarn (40-60 yds)
- Yellow, Red, Green, and Brown
- I used Lily Sugar'n Cream
- G 4.0 mm hook
- Yarn needle
- Scissors
- Keyring (with chain recommended)

Notes:

This pattern uses a Magic Circle. If you need help with this technique

Directions

Begin with yarn color for each section and G 4.0 mm hook

SHELL:
- Finished size should be approximately 3" wide and 3" tall.
- Use Yellow yarn and G 4.0 mm hook
- Begin with Magic Circle or ch 2 and work into the 2nd ch from
- hook
- Leave a long beginning tail for stitching the Taco together.

Round 1: ch 2 (counts as 1st hdc here & throughout), 9 hdc in magic circle, sl st into top of beg ch (10 hdc)

Round 2: ch 2, hdc in same, 2 hdc in next st, 9 times, sl st into top of beg ch (20 hdc)

Round 3: ch 2, hdc in same, hdc in next, *2 hdc in next, hdc in next," 9 times, sl st into top of beg ch (30 hdc)

Round 4: ch 1, *sc in next 2, 2 sc in next,* 10 times, sl st into top of beg ch, FO and leave a long tail for sewing to the rest of the taco. FO leaving a long end tail also. See Finishing Instructions (p. 7).

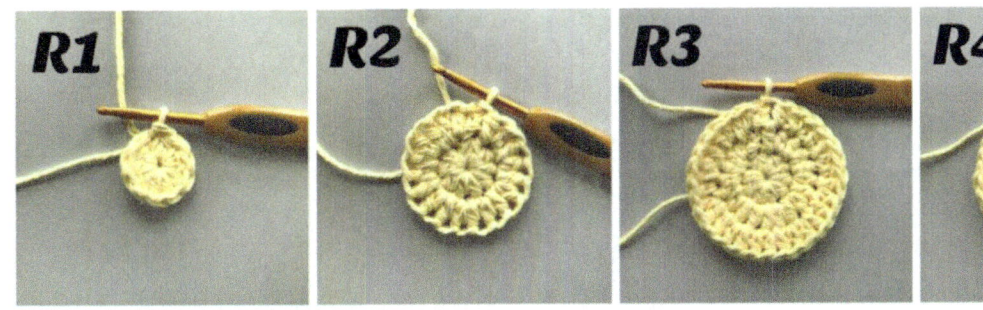

MEAT:

The finished size should be approximately 2.75" wide and 1.5" tall.
- Use Brown yarn and G 4.0 mm hook
- Begin with Magic Circle or ch 2 and work into the 2nd ch from
- hook

Round 1: ch 2 (counts as 1st hdc here & throughout), 9 hdc in magic circle, sl st into top of beg ch (10 hdc)

Round 2: ch 2, hdc in same, 2 hdc in next st, 9 times, sl st into top of beg ch (20 hdc)

Round 3: ch 2, hdc in same, hdc in next, *2 hdc in next, hdc in next," 9 times, sl st into top of beg ch (30 hdc)

Round 4: ch 1, fold circle in half with ch 1 at the edge, sl st into BLO of both the edges (center 2 loops), ch 1, *sl st into next to BLO st, ch 1,* through each pair of loops across (15 sl st + ch 1) FO leaving a long tail.

LETTUCE:
- The finished size should be approximately 3"wide and 1.75" tall.
- Use Green yarn and G 4.0 mm hook
- Begin with Magic Circle or ch 2 and work into the 2nd ch from hook

Round 1: ch 2 (counts as 1st hdc here & throughout), 4 hdc in magic circle, (5 hdc)

Round 2: ch 2, turn, hdc in same st, 2 hdc in next st, 2 hdc in next 3 st, *final st(s) of round will be placed in top ch of prev round that served as 1st hdc here & throughout* (10 hdc)

Round 3: ch 2, turn, hdc in same st, hdc in next, *2 hdc in next, hdc in next,* 3 times (15 hdc)

Round 4: ch 1, turn skip 1st st, 4 sc in each st next 12, skip next, sl st into last st. (48 sc) FO leaving a long tail.

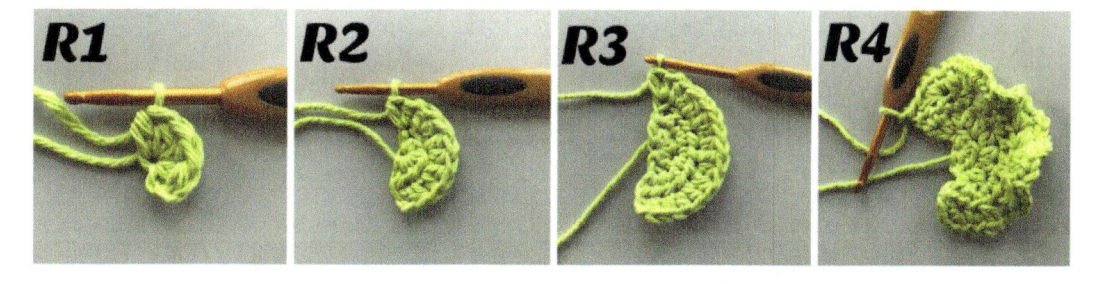

TOMATO:
- Finished size should be approximately 2.5"wide and 1.5" tall.
- Use Red yarn and G 4.0 mm hook
- Begin with Magic Circle or ch 2 and work into the 2nd ch from hook

| 75

TOMATO:

Round 1: ch 2 (counts as 1st hdc here & throughout), 4 hdc in magic circle, (5 hdc)

Round 2: ch 2, turn, hdc in same st, 2 hdc in next st, 2 hdc in next 3 st, *final st(s) of round will be placed in top ch of prev round that served as 1st hdc here & throughout* (10 hdc)

Round 3: ch 2, turn, hdc in same st, hdc in next, *2 hdc in next, hdc in next,* 3 times (15 hdc)

Round 4: ch 1, turn, sl st into each st across, (15 sl st)

Round 5: ch 1, turn, sl st into of each st across, sl st into top of beg ch and FO, leaving a long end. See photos below for stitch placement detail. (15 sl st)

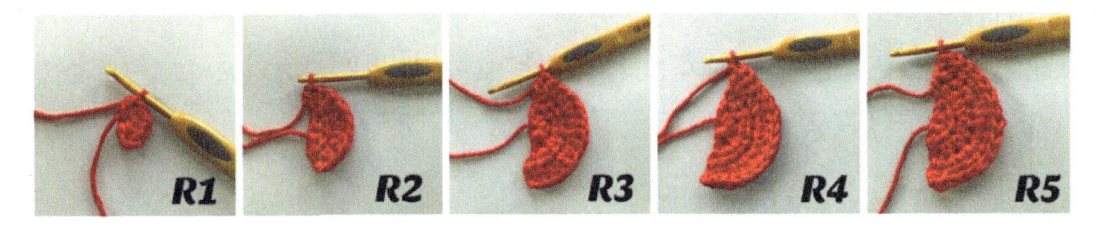

R5 STITCH PLACEMENT: Place 1st sl st into single loop of current stitch. Place all other sl sts of round into the 2 loops of each st that are toward the front. Reference photos below for detail.

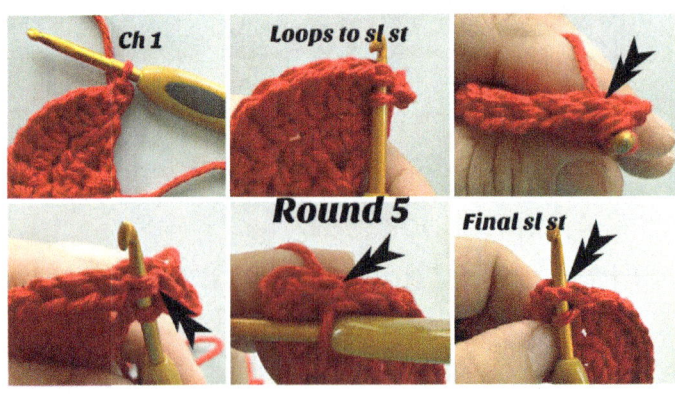

FINISHING TACO KEYCHAIN:

Stitch the Lettuce, Tomato, and Meat together:
- Weave in all but one end of the Lettuce, Tomato, and Meat pieces.
- Stack the pieces: Lettuce on bottom, Meat in the middle, Tomato on top.
- Use the remaining yarn end to stitch the pieces together along the bottom edge. Weave in the final yarn end.

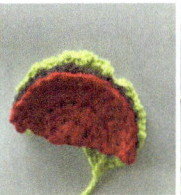

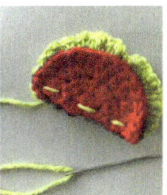

Stitch the Fillings into the Taco Shell:
Open the taco shell with the wrong side up. Place the filling pieces on one half, then bring the other half up to meet it, tugging if necessary. Pin or hold the shell in place and use the yarn ends to stitch it together, starting at one edge. Secure the lower curve first, then stitch around the entire edge at R4 to finish.

Adding a Keyring to your Taco Keychain:
Simply insert a split key ring or jump ring into one of the stitches from your initial magic circle on the top of the key ring. Secure. That's it! Enjoy your taco!

| 77

Other keychain patterns ideas

Camera keychain

LEVEL: EASY

Materials

- Yarn: Schachermayr Catania. (White, brown, yellow, pink, blue, red, black or anything you like)
- Hook: 2,5 mm
- Safety eyes

Directions

LENSE:
Start with a soft pink color
1. row: magic ring and 6 sc into it.
2. row: 2sc in each st around (12)
3. row: (sc in next st, 2sc in next st)*6 (18)
4. row: (sc in each of next 2 sts, 2sc in next st)*6 (24) change to white color 5. row: sc in next st, 2sc in next st, (sc in each of next 3 sts, 2sc in next st)*5, sc in each of next 2 sts (30) 6. row: (sc in each of next 8 sts, sc2tog)*3 (27)---slst into next st and cut the yarn leaving long yarntail for sewing.

Directions

CAMERA BODY:
1. ch20, from 2nd st from hook 18 sc, 3sc to the last st, back on the other side of chain 18 sc, 2sc to the last st, slst to the first st of row.
2. crochet only into the back loops in this row. Ch1, sc in each st around, slst to first st (41)
3-5. Ch1, sc in each st around, slst to first st (41) change color
6-8. Ch1, sc in each st around, slst to first st (41) change back to original color
9-12. Ch1, sc in each st around, slst to first st (41) change color to the top color of the camera
13-14. Ch1, sc in each st around, slst to first st (41)
15. crochet only into the back loops this row. Sc2tog, sc in each of next 17 sts, sc3tog, sc in each of next
17 sts, sc2tog. (37)---slst into next st and cut the yarn leaving long yarntail for sewing.

CAMERA BUTTON: ch4 and starting from the 3rd st from hook hdc in each of next 2 sts.--- cut the yarn leaving long yarntail for sewing.

HANGER: ch16, from the 2nd st from hook slst 15 times, cut yarn leaving long yarntail for sewing.

- *Attach the safety eye, and embroider some cute kawaii face details onto the lense, than sew it up on the camera body. Fill the camera body with just a little bit of fiberfill, than sew the top edges together. You may use only the front loops of sts by sewing. Sew up the camera button on the top of the camera. Sew up the hanger on the corner of the camera.*

Sun Keychain

LEVEL: EASY

Materials

- DK weight yarn in yellow, orange and pink (I used Paintbox Yarns Cotton DK in Buttercup Yellow, Mandarin Orange and Bubblegum Pink)
- 2.5mm crochet hook
- 8mm safety eyes
- Polyester Fiberfill
- Black embroidery floss
- Keychain
- Stitch marker, yarn needle, scissors

Special Stitches

Double crochet 4 together (dc4tog): [Yarn over, insert hook in stitch, yarn over and pull up a loop, yarn over and pull through 2 loops] x4, yarn over and draw through all 5 loops on hook.

| 81

Yarn Notes:

- The finished item measures approximately 2.5" x 2.5" (6.5cm x 6.5cm) when using the materials listed.
- Pieces are worked in a continuous spiral starting with a magic ring unless otherwise specified. Mark the first stitch of each round with a removable stitch marker.
- Gauge is not important in this pattern. Use a hook size to match your chosen yarn. Make sure that your stitches are tight enough to prevent stuffing from showing through and adjust hook size if necessary.

Directions:

Sun (make 2, yellow)

R1: 6 sc in magic ring (6)
R2: [Inc] x6 (12)
R3: [Sc, inc] x6 (18)
R4: Sc, inc, [2 sc, inc] x5, sc (24)
R5: [3 sc, inc] x6 (30)
R6: 2 sc, inc, [4 sc, inc] x5, 2 sc (36)
R7: [5 sc, inc] x6 (42)
Fasten off invisibly and weave in ends on both pieces.

Cheeks (make 2, pink)

R1: 6 sc in magic ring (6)
Fasten off invisibly leaving a long tail for sewing.

Directions:

Face
- Taking one of the yellow pieces, insert the safety eyes between R3 and R4, making sure that they are in line with each other on either side of the magic ring. Trim stems off the back of the eyes.
- Sew the cheeks below the eyes over R5 and R6.
- Use a small amount of black embroidery floss to sew a little mouth.

Rays (orange)

Place the two yellow pieces wrong sides together with the face details facing up.

Join orange yarn in any st. Ch 1, sc in same st. [Ch 3, dc4tog in third chain from hook, sc in next 3 sts] x 13, ch 3, dc4tog in third chain from hook, sc in last 2 sts (14 dc4tog + 42 sc)

Start stuffing when you're 3/4 of the way around. Continue to add small bits of stuffing as you go but avoid over stuffing.

Fasten off invisibly in the first sc of the round, weave in ends.

Using a long piece of yellow yarn, sew the keychain to the top just behind the rays. Now enjoy your cute keychain!

Toadstool Sweater Keychain

Materials

- DK Weight Yarn in sweater colour, red and white (I used Paintbox Yarns Cotton DK in Mustard Yellow/Soft Fudge, Pillar Red and Paper White)
- 4 ply yarn in white or white embroidery floss
- 2.5mm crochet hook
- Fabric glue
- Keychain (I used a 1" keychain ring with a 1.25" chain)
- Stitch marker, yarn needle, scissors

Notes:

The pattern is written using US terminology and measures approximately 2" x 3.5" (5cm x 9cm) when using the materials listed.

The body of the sweater is worked in joined rounds from the top down. The sleeves are added at the end and are worked in a continuous spiral without joining.

The ch 1 at the beginning of each round does not count as a stitch.

Gauge is not important in this pattern. However, using a different yarn and hook size will change the size and look of the finished item.

Directions

SWEATER BODY

R1: Ch 16, sl st to first ch without twisting

R2: Ch1, sc in same ch and in each ch around, sl st to first sc to join (16)

R3: Ch 1, [hdc-inc] x16, sl st to first hdc to join (32)

R4-5: Ch 1, [hdc] x32, sl st to first hdc to join (32)

R6: Ch 1, 5 hdc, sk 6, 10 hdc, sk 6, 5 hdc, sl st to first hdc to join (20)

R7-9: Ch 1, [hdc] x20, sl st to first hdc to join (20)

R10: Ch 1, [sc] x20 (20)

Fasten off invisibly to first sc and weave in ends.

SLEEVES

The sleeves are worked in a continuous spiral. Do not join at the end of each round.

LEFT SLEEVE

Join yarn to the first skipped st from R6 of the body.

R1: Ch 1, sc in same st, [sc] x5. Sc in both corner sts on the front and back of the sweater body (8) – see images below.

R2-7: [Sc] x8 (8). Fasten off invisibly and weave in the end.

RIGHT SLEEVE

Join yarn to the last skipped st from R6 of the body.

R1: Ch 1, sc in same st and both corner sts on the front and back of the sweater body, [sc] x5 (8)

R2-7: [Sc] x8 (8). Fasten off invisibly and weave in end.

Directions

NECKLINE (yellow)

Leaving a longer starting tail for attaching the keychain (approximately 4"/10cm), join yarn in the centre st at the back of the neck.

Ch 1, hdc in same st, hdc-dec, [2 hdc, hdc-dec] x3, hdc (12)

Fasten off invisibly to first hdc leaving a long tail of approximately 4"/10cm. Use the leftover yarn tails to attach the keychain. Weave in ends.

TOADSTOOL (starting with red)

R1: 5 sc in magic ring (5)

R2: Ch 1, turn. [Inc] x 5 (10)

Fasten off and weave in ends.

Join white yarn to the centre of the magic ring at the bottom of the toadstool (straight side). Ch 2, dc in same space. Fasten off and weave in ends.

Using 4 ply white yarn or white embroidery floss, make small stitches on the toadstool for the spots.

Fasten off and weave in ends.

Glue or sew the toadstool to the front of the sweater. The bottom of the toadstool should sit 3 rounds up from the bottom of the sweater.

School bus keychain

Materials

- 3.0 mm (C USA, 11 UK) Crochet Hook
- DK (3, Light) Yarn
- One Stitch Marker (to work in the round)
- Poly-Fil or Cotton Stuffing
- Tapestry Needle

Yarns & Colors

For my Schoolbus Amigurumi, I used Paintbox Yarns Cotton DK in the following colors:

A – Buttercup Yellow (423)
B – Marine Blue (434)
C – Stormy Grey (405)
D – Pure Black (402)
E – Rose Red (414)
F – Blood Orange (420)
G – Champagne White (403)

Size

3" (7 cm) in length, 1.5" (4 cm) in width, 1.5" (4 cm) tall.

Pattern notes

- If the pattern says "sc 2", it means that you have to crochet 1 sc into each of the next 2 sts.
- (...) – Repeat the instruction within brackets for the indicated number of times.
- [...] – Repeat the instruction within brackets all in the same indicated st.
- The stitch count is indicated within brackets at the end of each line of instructions.

Directions

REAR WINDOW
- With B, ch 6.
- Row 1. Sc 1 in the second ch from hook, sc 4. (5 sts)
- Row 2. Ch 1, turn. Sc 5. (5 sts)
- Fasten off leaving a long tail for sewing.

DOOR
- With B, ch 4.
- Row 1. Sc 1 in the second ch from hook, sc 2. (3 sts)
- Row 2-5. Ch 1, turn. Sc across. (3 sts)
- Fasten off leaving a long tail for sewing.

SIDE WINDOWS (Make 5)
With B, ch 4.
Row 1. Sc 1 in the second ch from hook, sc 2. (3 sts)
Row 2. Ch 1, turn. Sc 3. (3 sts)
Fasten off leaving a long tail for sewing.

Directions

MIRRORS
(Make 2)
With D, ch 2.
Fasten off leaving a long tail for sewing.

GRILL
With C, ch 4.
Row 1. Sc 1 in the second ch from hook, sc 2. (3 sts)
Row 2. Ch 1, turn. Sc 3. (3 sts)
Fasten off leaving a long tail for sewing.

WHEELS (Make 4)
With C, make a MC.
Round 1. Sc 6 in MC. (6 sts)
Close the round with an invisible join.
Join D in any st from round 1.
Round 2. Sc inc 6. (12 sts)
Join with an invisible join.
Fasten off leaving a long tail for sewing.

FRONT BUMPER
With D, ch 9.
Row 1. Sc 1 in the second ch from hook, sc 7. (8 sts)
Fasten off leaving a long tail for sewing.

REAR BUMPER
With D, ch 10.
Row 1. Sc 1 in the second ch from hook, sc 8. (9 sts)
Fasten off leaving a long tail for sewing.

SCHOOL BUS
(Work in the round)
With A, make a MC.
Round 1. Sc 6 in MC. (6 sts)
Round 2. Sc inc 6. (12 sts)
Round 3. ([Sc 3], sc 2) 4 times. (20 sts)
Round 4. Sc 1, ([sc 3], sc 4) 3 times, [sc 3], sc 3. (28 sts)
Round 5-17. Sc around. (28 sts)
Round 18. Sc 18, (BLO inv dec 1, BLO sc 1) 3 times, sc 1. (25 sts)
Round 19. Sc 1. Remove your hook and keep the st with a st marker (photo 1).

Directions

Windshield Decreases

Join new yarn in the 8th st from the end of round 18.

Row 1. Sc dec 4 (photo 2 shows the first dec. For clarity, this step is shown with yarn B).

Row 2. Ch 1, turn. Sc dec 2. Sl st into the same st where you joined.

Fasten off.

Start working again from the st you placed on the st marker at the beginning of the round.

Sc 17 (the last st goes into the same st where you joined the yarn for the decreases), sc 2 (over the last 2 decreases), sc 1 into the last st where you made a dec (photo 3). (21 sts)

Round 20-21. Sc around. (21 sts)
Start stuffing your school bus.

Round 22. (Inv dec 1, sc 5) 3 times. (18 sts)

Round 23. Sc all around. (18 sts)
Add more stuffing if needed.

Round 24. (Inv dec 1, sc 1) 6 times. (12 sts)

Round 25. Inv dec 6. (6 sts)
Fasten off and sew the opening by threading the yarn tail through the BLO of the sts from round 25.

Directions

ASSEMBLY

Front

Sew the windshield onto the windshield decreases of rounds 18-19.

Attach the grill on the top half of the front of the bus (rounds 23-24), and the front bumper around the bottom half.

Sew one mirror on each side of the windshield.

Using yarn E, F, and G, embroider the headlights on the sides of the grill, and warning lights just above the windshield.

Rear

On the back of the bus (rounds 1-4), sew the rear window and the rear bumper. Then, with short lengths of E, F, and G, embroider the rear lamps.

Sides Sew 3 side windows on one side of the bus, and 2 windows and the door on the other side. Attach the wheels by only sewing their top halves onto the bus. Cut approximately 9" (23 cm) of yarn D, and split the plys of the yarn in half in order to obtain a thinner thread and embroider two horizontal lines between the wheel and the windows.

Fasten off and weave in all your ends.

Your crochet school bus is ready!!!

Roller Skate Keychain

Materials

- Acrylic or Cotton yarn (sport weight) of 3 colors: blue, ecru and pink. 1 skein each will be more than enough.
- Some ecru DMC thread for embroidery (3 strands), 6 times 31 cm long
- A 4 mm and 1,75 mm crochet hooks
- 5 mm jump rings x6
- Polyester fiberfill for stuffing
- A keychain swivel clasp

Notes:

- Every row ends with a ch 1 then turn, and every round ends with a slip stitch. The whole pattern is made with the 4 mm hook except for the boot's eyelets, which are made with the 1,75 mm hook.
- The yarn gauge for this pattern is 5 cm x 5 cm = 10 stitches (sc) x 10 rows.

Directions:

The boot's sole

- Ch 13, starting the 2nd loop from the hook:
- Round 1: 11 sc, 4 sc in the last stitch, continue working on the other side of the chain base: 10 sc, (3 sc in the last stitch – which is the 1st one we worked in). (28)

Directions

The boot's sole:

Round 2: hdc inc, 3 hdc, 4 sc, 3 hdc, hdc inc, (1 sc, 1 hdc) in the next stitch, (1 hdc, 1sc) in the next stitch, hdc inc, 3 hdc, 4 sc, 3 hdc, hdc inc, 2 sc (34)

R3: 1 sc, hdc inc, 8 sc, 2 hdc, 3 sc, (1 sc, 1 hdc) in the next stitch, (1 hdc, 1 sc) in the next stitch, 3 sc, 2 hdc, 8 sc, hdc inc, 1 sc, sc inc x2 (40)

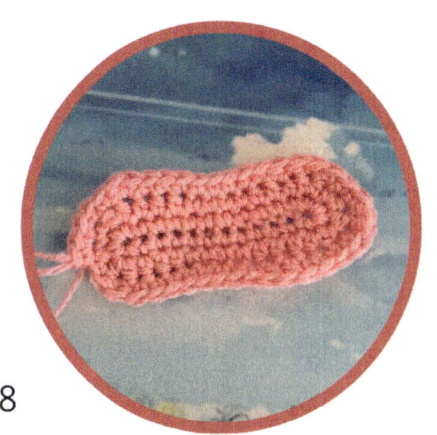

Here's the foundation for the boot's sole. Crochet two identical pieces following these instructions. For one piece, cut the yarn and secure it after completing round 3. Meanwhile, for the second piece, we'll continue building up the top of the boot from this base.

Switch to a new yarn color and continue crocheting on one of the sole pieces:

R4: Work this round in the Back Loops Only of the stitches: 2 sc, sc inc, 13 sc, sc inc, 2 sc, sc inc, 13 sc, sc inc, 6 sc (44)

R5 to 7: 44 sc (44)

R8: 14 sc, sc dec, 3 sc, (sc dec) x 3, 3 sc, sc dec, 14 sc (39)

R9: 13 sc, sc dec, sc3tog, sc dec, sc3tog, sc dec, 12 sc, sc dec (31)

Cut the yarn and make an invisible join to finish the round.

Directions

The boot's sole:

Identify the three middle stitches that form the rounded front of the boot and leave them unworked. Join the yarn with a single crochet decrease on the right side of the boot, commencing with the first available stitch after the three middle stitches. And now we're going to work in rows:

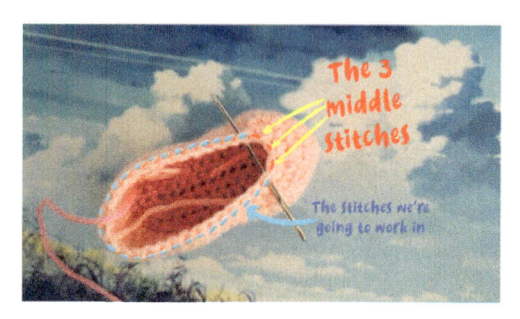

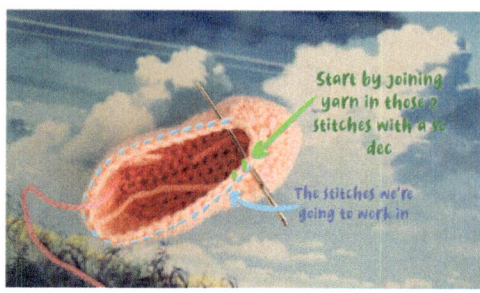

Row 10: sc dec (the one we did to join the yarn back), 24 sc, sc dec (26)

R11: sc3tog, 20 sc, sc3tog (22)

R12: sc3tog, 16 sc, sc3tog (18)

R13: sc dec, 14 sc, sc dec (16)

R14: 16 sc (16)

R15: 5 sc, sc dec, 2 sc, sc dec, 5 sc (14)

Chain 1 and proceed to outline the rows we've previously crocheted. This step is crucial for establishing the framework where the eyelets, the openings for the laces, will be situated. Do as follow: ch1, 6 sc, 3 sl st in the 3 central stitches we left unworked, 6 sc, chain 1 then cut the yarn and make an invisible join to finish the row.

After completing the boot, take the second sole we've made earlier and sew it underneath the boot, combining it with the first sole to add thickness to it.

Directions

The tongue of the boot

Ch4, starting the 2nd loop from the hook:

Row 1: 3 sc (3)

Row 2: 1 sc, sc inc, 1 sc (4)

R3: 1 sc, (sc inc) x 2, 1 sc (6)

R4 to 9: 6 sc (6)

R10: sc dec, 2 sc, sc dec (4)

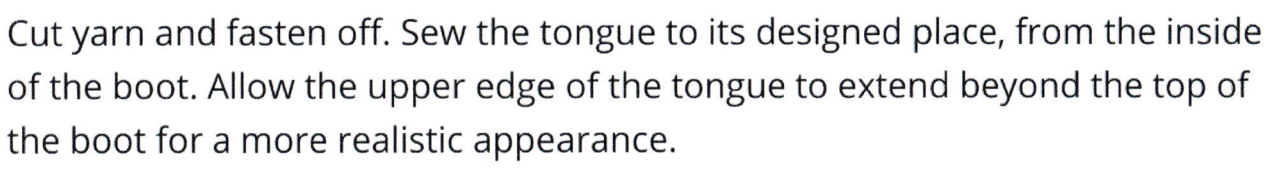

Cut yarn and fasten off. Sew the tongue to its designed place, from the inside of the boot. Allow the upper edge of the tongue to extend beyond the top of the boot for a more realistic appearance.

The Top Closure of the Boot

To secure the top of the boot after stuffing it with polyester fiber, we need to make a tiny piece to sew inside, grab your hook and with the same color as your boot:

Ch6, starting the 2nd loop from the hook:

Row 1 to 3: 5 sc (5)

R4: sc dec, 1 sc, sc dec (3)

R5: sc3tog (1)

Cut the yarn and leave a tail for sewing.

| 95

Directions

The heel

Make a magic circle.

Round 1: 4 sc (4)

Round 2: 3 sc in each stitch (so 3 sc x 4) (12)

R3: sc inc, 3 sc, (3 sc in the next stitch), 2 sc, (3 sc in the next stitch), 3 sc, sc inc (18)

R4: BLO: 2 sc, sc inc, 12 sc, sc inc, 2 sc (20)

R5: 6 hdc, 1 sc, 6 sl st, 1 sc, 6 hdc (20)

Cut the yarn and leave a tail for sewing. Sew the heel to the boot by sewing the rounded part onto the corresponding rounded section of the sole. Ensure the flat part is oriented towards the front of the shoe. Don't forget to fill the inside of the boot with some polyester fiber.

The plate of the skate

Ch14, starting the 2nd loop from the hook:

Round 1: 12 sc, 3 sc in the last stitch, continue working on the other side the chain base: 11 sc, 2 sc in the last stitch (28)

Round 2: hdc inc, 2 hdc, 1 sc, 4 sl st, 1 sc, hdc inc, 2 hdc, 1 sc, (3 hdc in the next stitch), 1 sc, 2 hdc, hdc inc, 1 sc, 4 sl st, 1 sc, 2 hdc, hdc inc, 1 sc (34)

Cut the yarn and leave a tail for sewing. This is the sole part for the plate.

| 96

Directions

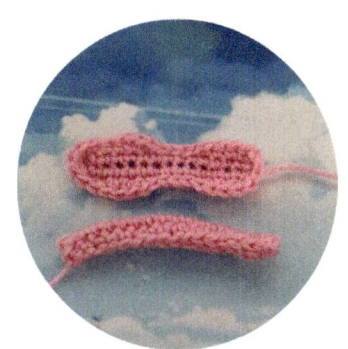

The plate of the skate

Grab your hook and yarn again and ch17, starting the 2nd loop from the hook:

Round 1: 15 sc, 3 sc in the last stitch, continue working on the other side the chain base: 14 sc, 2 sc in the last stitch (34)

Round 2: 34 sc (34)

Cut the yarn and fasten off. Take this piece, fold it in 2 and sew the top side together. After that, sew this to the plate's sole we just made.

The wheels and the truck axles

The truck axles

Note that they should be the same color as the plate.
Make a magic circle.
Round 1 to 4: 6 sc (6)
Cut yarn and leave a tail for sewing. Make 4 of them.

The Wheels

Make a magic circle.
Round 1: 6 sc (6)
Round 2: sc inc x 6 (12)
R3: FLO 12 sc (12)
R4: 12 sc (12)
R5: BLO: (1 sc, sc inc) x6 (18)
R6: BLO 18 sc (18)
R7 to 8: 18 sc (18)
R9: BLO: (1 sc, sc dec) x6 (12)
R10: sc dec x 6 (6)

Directions

The Wheels

Cut the yarn and leave the middle hole open. Make 4 of them. Insert the top of a truck axle into the designated hole and, sew the wheel together with the truck. Do this to the 4 wheels. Then sew the 4 truck axles (and wheels) to the skate's plate.

The Toe Stop

Make a magic circle.
Round 1: 5 sc (5)
Round 2: sc inc x 5 (10)
Round 3: 10 sc (10)

R4: 1 sc, sc dec, 2 sc, sc dec, 1 sc, sc dec (7) Add 1 sc, then sc dec after round 4 then cut the yarn. Slightly fill the toe stop with some polyester fiber, then sew it on the front of the roller's plate. Sew the plate beneath the boot by sewing the front of the boot to the front of the plate and the heel to the back of the plate. However, refrain from sewing the middle of the boot directly onto the plate; maintain a gap to ensure that the middle section of the boot does not come into contact with the plate. This method ensures proper assembly while preserving the distinct shape of the boot.

| 98

Directions

The Pull Loop

Ch7, starting the 2nd loop from the hook:

Round 1: 5 sc, (3 sc in the last stitch), continue working on the other side of the chain base: 4 sc, (2 sc in the last stitch) (14)

Cut the yarn. Sew the top and bottom to fashion it into a shoe's pull loop. Attach the keychain in it. Then sew the pull loop behind the boot, the rounded part being at the top.

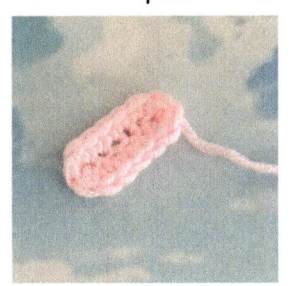

The boot's eyelets

Gather your jump rings, a 1.75 mm crochet hook, and the DMC thread (using 3 strands). Begin by making a slipknot and joining the yarn to the jump ring with a single crochet. Work single crochets around the jump ring until it's fully covered. Conclude with an invisible join and fasten off. Repeat this process six times in total. Finally, meticulously sew the six eyelets into their designated positions on the boot, 3 on each side. The final touch, if you desire, is to embellish the eyelets with a charming ribbon lace.

Thank you!

Dear Reader,

As we reach the end of "Tiny Treasures: A Crochet Guide to Adorable Keychains," I want to extend my deepest gratitude for choosing this book and joining me on this creative adventure. Your interest and dedication to crafting these charming keychains bring life to the patterns and designs shared within these pages.

Crocheting is not just a hobby; it's an art form that thrives on patience, practice, and a sprinkle of creativity. Every stitch you make is a step towards mastering this beautiful craft, and every finished piece is a testament to your perseverance and imagination.

Remember, the most wonderful creations often come from moments of trial and error. Embrace each mistake as a learning opportunity and each success as a celebration of your growing skills. Allow your creativity to flow freely, and don't be afraid to experiment with colors, textures, and designs to make each keychain uniquely yours.

Thank you for your time, effort, and enthusiasm. I hope this book has inspired you and added joy to your crochet journey. Keep creating, keep exploring, and most importantly, keep enjoying the process.

With heartfelt appreciation,

Printed in Great Britain
by Amazon